Learn Italian Like a Native *for Beginners*

COLLECTION

Learning Italian in Your Car Has Never Been Easier! Have Fun with Crazy Vocabulary, Daily Used Phrases, Exercises & Correct Pronunciations

www.LearnLikeNatives.com

© Copyright 2021 By Learn Like A Native

ALL RIGHTS RESERVED

No part of this book may be reproduced, stored in a retrieval system, or transmitted in any form or by any means, without the prior written permission of the publisher.

Table of Contents

INTRODUCTION 1

WHY LEARN ITALIAN IS, A GOOD CHOICE 5

CHAPTER 1 – THE FIRST IMPRESSION IS VERY IMPORTANT 11

CHAPTER 2 – ARE WE RELATED? 22

CHAPTER 3 – WHAT DAY IS IT? 30

CHAPTER 4 – THERE IS NO GIFT LIKE THE PRESENT. 42

CHAPTER 5 – HAVE A LOOK AROUND 55

CHAPTER 6 – HOW FAR CAN YOU COUNT? 63

CHAPTER 7 – WHAT DID YOU WANT TO BE WHEN YOU GREW UP? 72

CHAPTER 8 – WHERE ARE WE GOING? 82

CHAPTER 9 – SURVIVAL 101 89

CHAPTER 10 – WHAT IS THE COLOR OF THE SKY? 95

CHAPTER 11 – SO MUCH TO DO, SO MUCH TO SEE 101

CHAPTER 12 – I AM A BIT HUNGRY 111

CONCLUSION 124

.... 127

CHAPTER 1 – DREAMING OF THE SOUTH 135

CHAPTER 2 – NOT ONLY BIRDS CAN FLY 152

CHAPTER 3 – DO YOU NEED A RIDE? 160

CHAPTER 4 – I AM HAPPY WHEN THE SUN IS SHINING 171

CHAPTER 5 – I HAVE SO MANY STORIES TO TELL 179

CHAPTER 6 – SO MANY ROADS AND SO MANY PLACES 204

CHAPTER 7 – EAT, TRAVEL, LOVE 213

CHAPTER 8 – BEING SICK ABROAD! 222

CHAPTER 9 – LEARN THE ROPES 228

CHAPTER 10 – LEARN, LEAD, INVEST 237

CHAPTER 11 – NEW JOB, NEW LIFE 248

CHAPTER 12 – BRING HOME THE BACON 256

CONCLUSION 264

Learn Italian Like a Native *for Beginners - Level 1*

Learning Italian in Your Car Has Never Been Easier! Have Fun with Crazy Vocabulary, Daily Used Phrases, Exercises & Correct Pronunciations

www.LearnLikeNatives.com

Introduction

If you have always wanted to learn Italian, you are not alone. According to the most recent statistics, Italian is the fourth most studied language in the world, with more and more people getting seduced by the language and its culture every single day.

Art, history, fashion, and design are just few of the reasons to study this beautiful, melodic language.

There is no right way to learn a new language. With so many options available, it is not surprising you might feel overwhelmed when choosing a learning style or method!

You probably have many questions; maybe you have no idea even where to start, and you are wondering if it's worth it. Well, I can guarantee you that learning Italian it's more than worth the effort! We will be right here to help and support you in this adventure and, thanks to the right tools and technology, your efforts will pay off quickly.

According to researches and studies conducted on people who speak and study Italian as non-native, the best and fastest way to learn this language is not to study grammar (as you may have guessed). Instead, it is much useful to study, recognize, and use selected keywords in everyday life and to reinforce your vocabulary through guided discussions and conversations.

Learning a new language is a long, gradual process. It is a far too big task to tackle all at once, and therefore we have broken it down into a series of lessons.

Multiple skills, as well as patience, are required to learn how to speak confidently and fluently, write a text to a friend, or watch an Italian TV series.

Most people who have only studied Italian through grammar books often struggle to speak the language in real life. Thanks to my method, you will speedily progress and feel more confident speaking Italian with a native.

In the audiobook format, the lessons are narrated by an Italian native speaker, so you can also grasp the proper diction while learning the language. Learn Italian by completing a series of interactive lessons: you won't just passively listen, but you will be encouraged to speak, repeat and perfect your pronunciation by comparing with native speakers. Thanks to the audiobook and its PDF version attached, you will be able to both train your ears or read and learn the spelling.

The best thing about this book is by far the flexibility it gives you to learn whenever and wherever you want! Our bite-sized lessons take roughly 20 to 30 minutes to complete and can be squeezed into your already busy schedule, whether you're sitting in your car or waiting for dinner to be ready.

With this book, you can choose the topic that is more relevant to you and your interests. Are you about to go on holiday? Look at the section dedicated to travel. Do you need to refresh your Italian for an upcoming business meeting? Our lessons have you covered: you can learn Italian anytime, anywhere.

What is the use of learning a new language and then forget it because you never get to use it in real life? For this reason, this book has been optimized to help you retain as much information as possible. Take advantage of micro-learning. You can start to practice what you will learn in our lessons: writing, listening, and speaking.

www.LearnLikeNatives.com

The goal of learning any language is to be able to conversate with native speakers. Therefore, a book for language learning should allow you to achieve this objective. While it is surely important to practice with discipline and devotion, to succeed, you will also need an effective plan to help you along the way.

Fortunately, this book has been studied by capable language experts, educators, and designers who know everything you need to make the most of learning a new language. We guaranteed a high-quality Italian learning experience that is interesting, and yes, even fun...!

Why Learn Italian is, a good choice

First of all, studies and researches show that learning a new language is a really good exercise for your brain and helps to improve your memory.

Italian is the fourth most studied language in the whole world, with more and more people getting seduced every single day. This is not surprising, considering its link to art, culture, fashion, and food just to name a few.

Wanting to travel to Italy is definitely one of the main reasons why people decide to learn Italian. Italy is one of the most beautiful and historically rich places in the world and, according to UNESCO, most of the world's cultural heritage sites are here located.

Learning a new language should always be about communication. The best way to make any experience abroad truly memorable is to speak a bit of the local language. By doing so, you will be able to communicate with the locals and create deeper connections. Speaking the same language means you can understand each other better. And trust me, this is going to make the time you spend away much easier and, more importantly, it will give you the chance to really immerse yourself in another culture.

Another thing to consider is that nowadays, every place is filled with Italian restaurants. Learning Italian will give you the chance to understand better their culinary tradition better and – more importantly – what you are eating. For example, did you know that there is a kind of pasta called "farfalle", which literally translates to "butterflies"?

And how can we forget the musicality and the charm of its words? It is a melodic language. A real pleasure to listen to!

You would also be pleased to know that Italian is much easier to learn than other languages. There are no silent letters or missing sounds and it is a completely phonetic language. This means that, once you know the alphabet and learn a few rules, you will be able to read and perfectly pronounce every single word. Moreover, as both English and Italian have Latin roots, some of the words and sounds are either the same or very similar. That's just amazing, right?

If you are a lover of classical music, you will surely know that many operas were composed in Italian. Just think about Giuseppe Verdi or Giacomo Puccini.

Or maybe you are passionate about fashion and have always dreamed of going to Milan's fashion week. In Italy, you will find the most prestigious fashion houses, like Armani, Dolce & Gabbana, Prada, and Versace, to name a few.

Whatever is your reason or motivation to learn Italian, we will be with you every step of the way.

www.LearnLikeNatives.com

FREE BOOK!

Get the *FREE BOOK* that reveals the secrets path to learn any language fast, and without leaving your country.

Discover:

- The **language 5 golden rules** to master languages at will

- Proven **mind training techniques** to revolutionize your learning

- A complete step-by-step guide to **conquering any language**

www.LearnLikeNatives.com

www.LearnLikeNatives.com

www.LearnLikeNatives.com

Chapter 1 – The first impression is very important

Everyone knows the old saying, "you only get one chance to make a first impression".

Therefore, it's no surprise that one of the first things every child learns is to say hello and introduce themselves. Even J.K. Rowling, the famous author of that young wizard's adventures, said "A good first impression can work wonders", and I completely agree.

Just a simple "Hello" can make all the difference in a conversation. That's exactly the reason why we will begin this exciting adventure with the Italian greetings. You will learn how to introduce yourself and greet people at different times of the day, among other useful things.

We will start with the most popular greetings. There are several ways to greet people in Italian, depending on who you are addressing and whether you want to be formal or not.

Ready to start? I really hope you are as excited as I am!

So, let's begin with the most common ways to greet someone in Italian:

Hello.	Ciao

Chow

The word "Ciao" is probably one of the most popular Italian words, now used as a friendly salutation around the world. It is an informal greeting that can be used at any time of the day for both "Hello" and "Goodbye". It is considered highly informal and used among people who already know each other pretty well.

Least known but very useful is another salutation:

Hello.	Salve

Sahl-veh

When you are unsure of how to greet people, it is better to use this formal version for "Hello". It comes from Latin, meaning 'to be well'. More polite than "ciao", it is preferable to use between colleagues or strangers.

Good morning.	Buongiorno

Bwohn-johr-noh

Literally translated "Buongiorno" means "good day". It's slightly more formal and common between strangers, but it would not be a problem if you use this to greet someone you already know. It is also used as a greeting upon waking up. You can use it both in the morning and in the afternoon.

As in English, also in Italian the greetings change depending on the time of the day. As such, in the afternoon, you can switch to:

| Good afternoon. | Buon pomeriggio |

Bwohn poh-meh-rih-joh

"Buon pomeriggio" (Good afternoon) exists in Italian. However, it would sound a bit odd if you greeted people saying this as it is not that common. Generally, native speakers will keep using "Buongiorno" also in the afternoon.

As the afternoon sets in, you should say "Good evening".

| Good evening. | Buona sera |

Bwoh-nah-seh-rah

You can use this greeting on both formal and informal occasions, but remember that it is only used when you are arriving.

Finally, when it's bedtime, you will say:

| Good night. | Buona notte |

Bwoh-nah-noht-teh

Remember! You should use "Buona notte" only when you are saying goodbye late at night and, as such, implying that you or your party are going to bed. It is also used to wish sweet dreams.

Last one. When departing you can simply use "Ciao" or the more polite salutation for Goodbye:

Goodbye.	Arrivederci

Ahr-ree-veh-dehr-chee

As for Goodbye, you can use both "Ciao" or "Arrivederci" (recommended for more formal occasions). It is similar to the word "aloha". As you may know, Hawaiians only use one word for both "hello" and "goodbye", which is "aloha". In a similar way, also in Italian most greetings can be used for both hello and goodbye.

You should also remember that, depending on whether you are greeting a friend or a stranger, you would use a different salutation.

For example, when entering a restaurant in the evening (or in any other formal occasion), you will say "Buona sera" if you want to sound polite. Although you can use "Ciao" if you are meeting some old friends or greeting someone you already know (informal occasion).

Farewell.	Addio.
Farewell. I love you.	**Addio**. Ti amo.

Ah-dee-oh

"Addio" is used as a final salutation when you are pretty sure you are not going to see someone ever again. It's a phrase very rich in drama, sadness, or irony, depending on the cases.

There is also a more informal version of "Arrivederci":

See you later.	Ci vediamo
Great! **See you later.**	Perfetto! **Ci vediamo.**

Cee veh-dihah-moh

How is your pronunciation? I hope you are starting to make progress.

See you in a few.	Ci vediamo più tardi
Ok! **See you in a few.**	Okl! **Ci vediamo** più tardi.

Cee veh-dihah-moh pihyou tahr-dee

When greeting, you may also want to ask how someone is doing.

| How are you? | Come stai? |

Koh-meh-stahy

You may have noticed that there is no literal translation, and the word "you" is not translated. While in English the pronoun is always used, in Italian the ending of the verb usually makes it clear who the subject is, so no pronoun is necessary.

Asking "Come stai?" is a really good way to start a friendly conversation. It is an informal greeting and can also be used between people you are familiar with to ask about their health or mood.

| How can I help you? | Come posso aiutarti? |

Koh-meh poos-soh ah-you-tahr-the

At this point, you have probably figured out the connection between two words: "how" and "come", and you know how important this word is in any language. Let's see another sentence that uses the word "Come":

| What is your name? | Come ti chiami? |

Koh-meh tee kyah-mee

To say what your name is in Italian you use:

My name is	Mi chiamo
My name is John.	**Mi chiamo** John.

Meek kyah-moh

I am	Io sono
I am new around here.	**Io sono nuovo** da queste parti.

Ih-oh Soh-noh

Thanks/Thank you.	Grazie.

Grah-tzee

"Grazie" is used to say both "thanks" or "thank you". However, if you wish to show more gratitude, you could say "many thanks," which translates to "Grazie mille" (literally a thousand thank yous).

Grah-tzee mih-leh

I am sorry.	Mi dispiace.

Mee dees-pyah-cheh

Nice to see you again.	Piacere di rivederti.

Pyah-cheh-reh dee ree-veh-dehr-tee

Was it too hard? Don't worry. Greetings are basic phrases you will need to memorize, but I promise that the upcoming sentences will be shorter and easier to remember.

What is new?	Che novità ci sono?

Che noh-vee-tah cee soh-noh

Another sentence with a similar meaning is "Cosa mi racconti?" What do you say?

Koh-sah mee rahc-chon-tee

How are you doing?	Come va?

Koh-meh vah

As you might know, "Ok" is an English expression. Nevertheless, it's universally used worldwide, even among Italian speakers. You should be aware, however, that there is an Italian equivalent as well:

Ok.	Va bene.

Vah beh-neh

How is it going? Are you finding it difficult, or is it easy? Maybe you need to practice a little bit more. Remember: practice is the key to mastery! Anyway, before we move to another topic, let's take a look at a short conversation that uses some of the words we have just learned.

Vendor	*Good morning!*
(Rivenditore):	Buongiorno.
John:	*Good morning to you, too.*
	Buongiorno anche a te.
Vendor:	*How can I help you?*
	Come posso aiutarti?

John:	*I am here to pick up a cake.*
	Sono qui per ritirare una torta.
Vendor:	*Sure. What is your name?*
	Certamente. Come ti chiami?
John:	*My name is John Hill.*
	Mi chiamo John Hill.
Vendor:	*Oh, I am sorry. Your bday cake is not ready yet.*
	Oh, mi dispiace. La tua torta di compleanno non è ancora pronta.
John:	*Ok. When can I come pick it up?*
	Va bene. Quando posso venire a ritirarla?
Vendor:	*It will be ready in one hour.*
	Sarà pronta in un'ora.
John:	*Great. I will run some errands and come back.*

	Fantastico. Vado a fare delle commisioni e torno.
Vendor:	*Thanks for understanding. See you in a few.*
	Grazie per la comprensione. Ci vediamo più tardi.
John:	*Sure. See you later!*
	Certo. A più tardi!

I hope you are not getting low blood sugar, because you will have to wait for a while. In the meantime, shall we go and learn some new words and phrases that relate to family and relatives? This could be really handy if you are going to have a birthday party!

Chapter 2 – Are we related?

I am sure your family would be pleased to tell you the story of your first word.

Language acquisition starts with receptive language, the understanding of sounds and words of the world around us. There is a good chance that either "mum" or "dad" (or a variable of these) was the first word you learned.

Dad	Papá
My **dad** went out to buy milk.	Mio **papá** è uscito a comprare il latte.

Pah-pà

Accent marks are very important in the Italian language. They can seem insignificant, but those tiny marks can completely change the meaning of a word. The accent on the à in "papà" - short on the first syllable and hard accent on the second - is fundamental as without it, you would be referring to the Pope (Papa).

Mom	Mamma

My **mom** is there, by the door.	Mia **mamma** è lì, vicino alla porta.

Mahm-mah

Son	Figlio
My **son** used to play tennis.	Mio **figlio** giocava a tennis.

Fee-glee-oh

Daughter	Figlia
My **daughter** likes to dance.	A mia **figlia** piace ballare.

Fee-glee-ah

In Italian, there are two genders: every noun must be either masculine or feminine. Figlio/Figlia is a good example. As an introductory guide, it is good to know that singular:

- Nouns ending in "o" are masculine (male), with few exceptions;
- Nouns ending in "a" are nearly all feminine (female).

Throughout this book, we will see several examples of these. As a general rule, you can form the feminine or masculine version of nouns changing the final vowel.

Therefore, you would use words like "figlia" or "questa" for female, and "figlio" or "questo" for male.

Brother	Fratello
This is my **brother** Alberto.	Questo è mio **fratello** Alberto.

Frah-teh-loh

Sister	Sorella
She is my **sister** Carla.	Lei è mia **sorella** Carla.

Soh-reh-lah

Uncle	Zio
I have two **uncles**.	Io ho due **zii**.

Zee-oh

Aunt	Zia
My **aunt** has two kids.	Mia **zia** ha due figli.

Zee-ah

While in English you can simply form the plurals by adding "s" at the end of every word, different rules apply in Italian. First of all, it is important to know the gender of the word: masculine or feminine. Then, to turn a singular word into a plural one, you usually need to change the final vowel as it follows:

- For nouns ending in "o" you will need to change the ending to "i" (Example: Zio – Zii)
- For nouns ending in "a" you will need to change the ending to "e" (Example: Zia –Zie)

But be careful, as there are some exceptions!

Cousin	Cugino
My **cousin** lives far away from here.	Mio **cugino** vive lontano da qui.

Cooh-jee-noh

Grandfather	Nonno
My **grandfather** has a good memory	Mio **nonno** ha una buona memoria.

Noh-noh

Grandmother	Nonna
My **grandmother** loved knitting.	Mia **nonna** amava lavorare a maglia.

Noh-nah

How is it going so far? Don't you worry, we just need to meet a few more people, and then we can take a short break.

Siblings	Fratello/Sorella
I have three **siblings**.	Io ho tre **fratelli/sorelle**.

Frah-teh-loh/Soh-reh-lah

Relatives	Parenti
I have many **relatives**.	Io ho molti **parenti**.

Pah-rehn-tee

Family	Famiglia
My **family** is big.	La mia è una **famiglia** numerosa.

Fah-mih-lih-ah

Neighbor	Vicino
Dan is a great **neighbor**.	Dan è un buon **vicino.**

Vee-cee-noh

Are you ready to use those words you have just learned? Great!

Allyson: *Happy birthday!*

Buon compleanno!

Kelly: *Hello! Thanks a lot! I am happy that you came.*

Ciao! Grazie mille! Mi fa piacere tu sia venuta.

Allyson: *I am happy that you invited me.*

Sono felice che tu mi abbia invitata.

Kelly: *Sure. Let me show you who everyone is.*

Certo. Lascia che ti mostri chi sono tutti.

Allyson: *Great!*

Fantastico!

Kelly: *That girl is my sister, and my cousin John is sitting next to her.*

Quella ragazza è mia sorella, e quello seduto di fianco a lei è mio cugino John.

Allyson: *Yeah. Next to them is your brother Mark, right?*

Si. Accanto a loro c'è tuo fratello Mark, giusto?

Kelly: *Perfect! Yes. He picks me up sometimes.*

Esatto! Si. A volte mi viene a prendere.

Allyson: *I remember.*

Me lo ricordo.

Kelly: *Good. By that other corner are grandma, grandpa, and uncle Ed.*

Bene. All'altro angolo ci sono nonna, nonno e zio Ed.

Allyson: *Your grandma looks so young!*

Tua nonna sembra così giovane!

Kelly: *Yes. I hope I have the same luck.*

Si. Spero avrò la stessa fortuna.

Allyson: *Don't we all?*

Non è quello che speriamo tutti?

Kelly: *Let's see... who's missing? Oh, well. Dad is outside, with the neighbors and the rest of the family.*

Vediamo… chi manca? Oh, ecco. Papá è fuori, con i vicini e il resto della famiglia.

Allyson: *Great! I can't wait to meet them.*

Ottimo! Non vedo l'ora di conoscerlo.

So, what do you think? Learning a new language is about listening to things over and over again and repeating many times. My advice is to always say the words out loud. This is an excellent way to practice a new language and, if you do so, you will see a significant improvement in the next chapters.

Chapter 3 – What day is it?

Learn how to measure and tell the time is hugely valuable. In many cultures, punctuality is extremely important and viewed as a form of respect, and I personally think it is a great sign of courtesy. Of course, you will also learn the days of the week and months, so you can make plans. Another thing you may want to know before leaving for a foreign country is what season is it, to know what to pack and dress accordingly.

As always, we will start with the basics:

Second	Secondo / Secondi
One minute has sixty **seconds**.	Un minuto ha sessanta **secondi**.

Seh-cohn-doh / Seh-cohn-dee

Minute	Minuto / Minuti
One hour has sixty **minutes**.	Un'ora ha sessanta **minuti**.

Mee-noo-toh / Mee-noo-tee

Hour	Ora / Ore

| There are twenty-four **hours** in a day. | Ci sono ventiquattro **ore** in un giorno. |

Oh-rah / Oh-reh

Great, let's carry on.

| Day | Giorno / Giorni |
| April has thirty **days**. | Aprile ha trenta **giorni**. |

Jorh-noh / Jorh-nee

| Week | Settimana / Settimane |
| We have one **week** to finish. | Finiamo tra una **settimana**. |

Seh-tee-mah-nah / Seh-tee-mah-neh

| Month | Mese / Mesi |
| We will be there next **month**. | Saremo lì il **mese** prossimo. |

Meh-seh / Meh-see

| Year | Anno / Anni |

| One more birthday, one more **year**. | Un altro compleanno, un altro **anno**. |

Ah-noh / Ah-nee

| Decade | Decennio |
| This **decade** is going to end soon. | Questo **decennio** sta per finire. |

Deh-chen-nioh

| Century | Secolo |
| This is the discovery of the **century**. | Questa è la scoperta del **secolo**. |

See-kol-oh

| Morning | Mattina |
| The meeting was this **morning**. | La riunione era questa **mattina**. |

Mah-tee-nah

| Afternoon | Pomeriggio |

Will you be there in the **afternoon**?	Sarai lì nel **pomeriggio**?

Poh-meh-ree-joh

Night	Notte
Moon comes out at **night**.	Di **notte** c'è la luna.

Noh-teh

Spring	Primavera
Everything flowers in **spring**.	Tutto fiorisce in **primavera**.

Pree-mah-veh-rah

Remember: the soft sound you need for "rah" will depend on the amount of air that you breathe out.

Summer	Estate
We had a fun **summer**.	Abbiamo passato un'**estate** divertente.

Ehs-tah-teh

Autumn	Autunno

| Look at the first **autumn** leaf. | Guarda le prime foglie d'**autunno**. |

How-tuh-noh

| Winter | Inverno |
| The **winter** is here. | E' arrivato l'**inverno**. |

In-vehr-noh

| January | Gennaio |
| **January** is the first month of the year. | **Gennaio** è il primo mese dell'anno. |

Jehn-nah-eeoh

At this point, you should know that, contrary to what happens in English, in Italian months and days of the week do not start with capital letters.

| February | Febbraio |
| That tree flowers in **February**. | Quell'albero fiorisce a f**ebbraio**. |

Feh-brah-yoh

March	Marzo
March is a good month for harvesting.	**Marzo** è un buon mese per il raccolto.

Marh-tzoh

April	Aprile
We stop activities on **April**.	Terminiamo le attività in **aprile**.

Ah-pree-leh

Have you noticed how most of the names of the months are similar between English and Italian? That's a relief, is it?

May	Maggio
May is going to be a great month.	**Maggio** sarà un mese fantastico.

Mah-joh

June	Giugno
The break starts on **June**.	Le vacanze iniziano a **giugno**.

Jooh-nyoh

July	Luglio
July is a hot month in Italy.	**Luglio** è un mese molto caldo in Italia.

Looh-lihoh

August	Agosto
This **August** will be rainy.	Questo **agosto** sarà piovoso.

Ah-goh-stoh

September	Settembre
Next semester starts in **September**.	Il prossimo semestre inizierà a **settembre**.

Seh-tehm-breh

October	Ottobre
We celebrated Halloween in **October**.	Noi festeggiamo Halloween in **ottobre**.

Oht-too-breh

November	Novembre

| My birthday is in **November**. | Il mio compleanno è a **novembre**. |

Noh-vehm-breh

| December | Dicembre |
| The year ends in **December**. | L'anno termina a **dicembre**. |

Dee-cehm-breh

| Monday | Lunedì |
| Today is **Monday**. | Oggi è **lunedì**. |

Loo-neh-dee

| Tuesday | Martedì |
| I have an appointment for next **Tuesday**. | Ho un appuntamento per **martedì** prossimo. |

Marh-teh-dee

Remember that the Italian "t" is pronounced very clear and strong, like the British one.

| Wednesday | Mercoledì |

| **Wednesday** is not a good day for me. | Il **mercoledì** per me non è una bella giornata. |

Mehr-ko-leh-dee

| Thursday | Giovedì |
| I'll see you next **Thursday**. | Ci vediamo **giovedì** prossimo. |

Joh-veh-dee

| Friday | Venerdì |
| The party is next **Friday**. | La festa è **venerdì** prossimo. |

Veh-nerh-dee

Please notice the grave accent mark on the words lunedì, martedì, mercoledì, giovedì, venerdì. The accent lets you know that, in these cases, the stress falls on the last syllable.

| Saturday | Sabato |
| I play football every **Saturday**. | Io gioco a calcio ogni **Sabato**. |

Sah-bah-toh

Sunday	Domenica
We can have breakfast this **Sunday**.	Possiamo fare colazione questa **Domenica**.

Doh-meh-nee-cah

How is it going? Are you ready for a short conversation?

Ally: *So, what are your plans for the next year?*

Quindi, che piani hai per il prossimo anno?

Juan: *I honestly don't know what will happen after the winter.*

Sinceramente non so cosa farò dopo l'inverno.

Ally: *Will you at least come back in February? The spring is lovely in here.*

Ma almeno ritornerai a febbraio? Qui la primavera è meravigliosa.

Juan: *If I don't, I promise I will be back to celebrate summer in July.*

Se non tornerò, prometto verrò per festeggiare l'estate a luglio.

Ally: *Everyone loves summer. I love autumn.*

Tutti amano l'estate. A me piace l'autunno.

Juan: *Why?*

Perchè?

Ally: *Leaves change colors, and I love the weather between September and November.*

Le foglie cambiano colore e amo il clima tra settembre e novembre.

Juan: Two weeks ago, you didn't love it that much.

Due settimane fa non ti piaceva così tanto.

Ally: Are you talking of that rainy Wednesday? I hated that.

Parli di quel mercoledì di pioggia? La odio.

Juan: Yeah. And it's even worse when it rains on Mondays.

Si. Ed è pure peggio quando piove di lunedì.

Ally: Oh, sure. I don't like Mondays. I love Fridays.

>   Oh, certo. Non mi piacciono i lunedì. Io amo i venerdì.

Juan: Like everyone. But I like Saturdays better.

>   Come tutti. Invece io preferisco i sabato.

Ally: Yes. Especially the ones in Spring, when you take your boat for a ride.

>   Si. Specialmente quelli in primavera, quando esci per un giro con la tua barca.

Juan: You remember it. Good.

>   Te lo ricordi. Brava.

It's not as hard as you thought, right? There is a lot to remember, but sometimes it's easier if you find the similarities between English and Italian, such as those in the names of the months. Again, practice makes perfect.

Now has come the time to learn some important verbs and how to conjugate them.

Chapter 4 – There is no gift like the Present

Just as in any other language, also in Italian verbs are an important part of everyday speaking. When studying a foreign language, the present is the first tense you will learn, as this will allow you to form simple sentences. It is used to describe something that is happening right now or a state of being. Using the present tense, you will be able to speak about your desires, interests, and plans.

First of all, in Italian, verb conjugation is done by changing the ending of the verb. Verbs are divided into 3 different categories, called "coniugazioni" - conjugations. Each one is characterized by a specific ending in its infinitive form:

- First conjugation: Verbs ending in -ARE (like amare)
- Second conjugation: Verbs ending in -ERE (like credere)
- Third conjugation: Verbs ending in -IRE (like partire)

In this chapter, I will teach you how to conjugate the regular verbs.

In addition, as you do in English, also in Italian you can merge all the 3rd person singular pronouns. For your convenience, this is what we will do here.

Hopefully, with a bit of practice, you will realize that Italian verb conjugation is actually much easier than it seems.

So, let's get started. There is no time like the present!

To love	Amare	Root	Termination
I love	Io amo	Am-	Are changes to "o"
You love	Tu ami		Are changes to "i"
He/She/It loves	Lui/Lei/Egli ama		Are changes to "a"
We love	Noi amiamo		Are changes to "iamo"
You love	Voi amate		Are changes to "ate"

| They love | Loro amano | | Are changes to "ano" |

The root of all regular verbs never changes. As you can see, the root is the part preceding the infinitive ending. So, for example, in "Amare" the root is "Am-". Like we said, the root always remains the same and different endings are added to denote the person, number or tense. Let's look at some examples.

I love the rain.	Io amo la pioggia.
She loves music.	Lei ama la musica.
You love movies.	Voi amate i film.
They love to play music.	Loro amano suonare.

Great! Here is a tip: using the above table, you will be able to conjugate every other regular verb that ends in "are". All you will have to do is add to the root the relevant ending, as we just did. Clearly, the same logic applies to the verbs of the second and third conjugation (-Ere and -Ire). That's good to know, right?

Here are a few more examples. For the verb "to sing" - "cantare", you can separate the root "Cant-", and all you will need to do is to add the correct ending, as previously explained. The root of the verb "to eat" – "mangiare" is "Mangi-", and for the verb "to share" - "condividere", the root is "Condivid-".

So, anyhow, what do you like to do in your free time? What are your interests? What are you passionate about? Come on, think about this for a moment. Verbs are important to discuss all of these things.

To believe	Credere	Root	Termination
I believe	Io credo	Cred-	Ere changes to "o"
You believe	Tu credi		Ere changes to "i"
He/She/It believes	Lui/Lei/Egli crede		Ere changes to "e"
We believe	Noi crediamo		Ere changes to "iamo"

You believe	Voi credete		Ere changes to "ete"
They believe	Loro credono		Ere changes to "ono"

You believe in loyalty.	Tu credi nella lealtà.
He only believes what is in front of his nose.	Lui crede solo a ciò che è davanti al suo naso.
You believe in yourselves.	Voi credete in voi stessi.
They believe in you.	Loro credono in te.

So, what have you learned, and what do you have faith in? Repeat with me: "io credo….". Eventually, you will be able to better express yourself in Italian, but –in the meantime- "io credo" is good enough.

Let's carry on with another important verb: "to leave" – "partire". In this case, the root is "Part-".

To leave	Partire	Root	Termination

I leave	Io parto		Ire changes to "o"
You leave	Tu parti		Ire changes to "i"
He/She/It leaves	Lei/Lui/Egli parte	Part-	Ire changes to "e"
We leave	Noi partiamo		Ire changes to "iamo"
You leave	Voi partite		Ire changes to "ite"
They leave	Loro partono		Ire changes to "ono"

I leave on a trip	Parto per un viaggio.
The train leaves at six.	Il treno parte alle sei.
We leave tomorrow.	Noi partiamo domani.

Now let's look at the present of the auxiliary verb "to be" – "essere". This verb is one of the most versatile, and you will use it a lot in Italian: to introduce yourself, find out more about something or someone, describe places and things, etc. It is an auxiliary verb and its purpose is to help other verbs conjugate in compound tenses. In other words, it helps to create more complex sentences and tenses.

There is also another verb that can sometimes be used with the same meaning of "to be": "stare" – "to stay". While in English "to stay" is only used to describe your location, in Italian, it can also be used to describe a state of being.

Here are some examples to explain the use of the verb "essere" (to be):

- To introduce yourself or describe something like nationality, profession, etc.: "You are Latin-American" –"Tu sei Latino Americano", "She is Lucy" –"Lei è Lucy", "I am a doctor" – "Io sono un medico"
- To describe something or someone. For example, "He is tall" – "Lui è alto", or "They are smart" – "Loro sono intelligenti".
- To speak about time and date, like "The meeting will be at seven" –"La riunione è alle sette", or "The dinner is ready" –"La cena è pronta".
- To talk about seasons and weather. For example "It is summer" –"E' estate".

Similarly, let's see when we should use the verb "stare" (to stay):

- To say or ask how someone is: "How are you?" – "Come stai?", "I'm fine" – "Sto bene".
- To give an order or exhortation: "Stay calm" – "Stai tranquillo".
- To explain where something is situated. "The house is on top of the mountain" –"La casa sta in cima alla montagna".
- To make continuous tenses or indicate an action. "I am studying" – "Sto studiando".

I know it may sound a bit confusing, but once you understand the differences, you will soon see how easy these are to use and how helpful they are to express yourself.

For the time being, let's see how to conjugate them.

To be	Essere	To stay	Stare	
I am	Io sono	I stay	Io sto	
You are	Tu sei	You stay	Tu stai	
He/She/It is	Lei/Lui/Egli è	He/She/It stays	Lei/Lui/Egli sta	

We are	Noi siamo	We stay	Noi stiamo	
You are	Voi siete	You stay	Voi state	
They are	Loro sono	They stay	Loro stanno	

Here are some examples of the "verbo essere".

I am a fan.	Io sono un tifoso.
She is a bit short.	Lei è piuttosto bassa.
The party is around nine.	La festa è intorno alla nove.
It is two in the morning.	Sono le due di mattina

We have described someone and talked about the time.

Now, let's see some examples of the "verbo stare".

You keep quiet.	Tu stai in silenzio.
She is crying.	Lei sta piangendo.

Be careful!	Stai attento!
They are unwell.	Loro stanno male.

Is everything clear? Don't worry! It will all become clear if you repeat it over and over again.

Alongside the verb "to be", the second most important verb in the Italian language is "to have" – "avere" –. It is an auxiliary and irregular verb that allows you to express numerous things: possessing something (literally or in a figurative way), communicate needs and desires, etc.

To have	**Avere**
I have	Io ho
You have	Tu hai
He/She/It has	Lei/Lui/Egli ha
We have	Noi abbiamo
You have	Voi avete

| They have | Loro hanno |

I have an appointment at eight.	Io ho un appuntamento alle otto.
It has big paws.	Ha grandi zampe.
We have a plan.	Noi abbiamo un piano.
They have a house by the lake.	Loro hanno una casa sul lago.

Are you looking forward to putting this into practice?

Emma: *Hi. I am Emma.*

Ciao. Io sono Emma.

David: *Nice to meet you. I am David.*

Piacere di conoscerti. Io sono David.

Emma: *Tell me, David. What do you like to do?*

Dimmi, David. Cosa ti piace fare?

David: *I enjoy sailing on weekends.*

Mi piace fare vela nel fine settimana.

Emma: *Do you have a boat?*

Hai una barca?

David: *Yes, I do. And what do you like to do?*

Si. E a te cosa piace fare?

Emma: *I have a dancing academy. I love to teach.*

Ho una scuola di danza. Io amo insegnare.

David: *Really? I have a niece. She loves to dance.*

Davvero? Io ho una nipote. Lei adora ballare.

Emma: *Great! How old is she?*

Fantastico! Quanti anni ha?

David: *She is 6 years old. Turns 7 in two weeks.*

Lei ha 6 anni. Ne compie 7 tra due settimane.

Emma: *I teach from 7. Maybe you could bring her.*

Io insegno a partire dai 7 anni. Magari potresti portarla.

David: *Awesome. I am sure she will love it.*

   Stupendo. Sono certo le piacerà molto.

As you can see, it is very important to know how to conjugate the Present simple. Just keep practicing until you achieve a better understanding.

www.LearnLikeNatives.com

Chapter 5 – Have a look around

Now, have a look around the room and tell me what you see. What's all around you? For instance, I usually keep a bottle of water on my desk, and I always carry my mobile phone and wallet. In this chapter, we will learn the names of a few things that you will probably have in your house.

Clock	Orologio
My **clock** says it is late.	Il mio **orologio** dice che è tardi.

Orh-roh-loh-joh

Remember what we said at the beginning about punctuality? You will need a "orologio" to be always right on time.

Light	Luce
Turn the **light** on.	Accendi la **luce.**

Loo-ceh

www.LearnLikeNatives.com

Money	Soldi
Spend your **money** wisely.	Spendi i tuoi **soldi** con saggezza

Sohl-dee

Bed	Letto
This **bed** is very comfortable.	Questo **letto** è molto comodo.

Leh-toh

Window	Finestra
That **window** points south.	Questa **finestra** si affaccia a sud.

Fih-nehs-trah

Water	Acqua
I want some **water**.	Voglio un pò di **acqua.**

Ah-kwah

www.LearnLikeNatives.com

Car	Auto
That is a nice **car.**	Quella è una bella **auto**.

How-toh

Bicycle	Bicicletta
I took your **bicycle.**	Ho preso la tua **bicicletta**.

Bee-cee-kleh-tah

Photo	Fotografia
I have your **photo** in my wallet.	Ho una tua **fotografia** nel mio portafoglio.

Foh-toh-grah-fee-ah

News	Notizie
Did you read the **news**?	Hai letto le **notizie**?

Noh-tee-zee-ah

"Notizie" are very important to keep you informed. Let me give you a little advice. When preparing to visit another country, you should start reading local news sources from that place a couple of weeks before you get there. That will give you an insight into what is happening in the country and – why not – also some great talking points when you are speaking with locals.

Bin	Cestino
I put it all in the **bin**.	Ho buttato tutto nel **cestino**.

Chehs-tee-noh

Toothbrush	Spazzolino da denti
I need a new **toothbrush**.	Ho bisogno di un nuovo **spazzolino da denti**.

Spah-tzoh-lee-noh dah dehn-tee

Mirror	Specchio
That **mirror** looks dirty.	Quello **specchio** sembra sporco.

Speh-keeoh

Laptop	(Computer) portatile
You can use my **laptop**.	Puoi usare il mio **portatile**.

Kom-pooh-terh por-tah-tee-leh

Computer	Computer
That is my **computer**.	Quello è il mio **computer**.

Kohm-pooh-terh

Cellphone	(Telefono) cellulare
I don't find my **cellphone**.	Non trovo il mio **cellulare**.

Cheh-loo-lah-reh

Id	Documento
Please, let me see your **id**.	Per favore, mostrami un tuo **documento**.

Doh-cooh-mehn-toh

Driving license	Patente di guida
You look funny in your **driving license**.	Sei buffo sulla tua **patente di guida**.

Pah-tehn-teh dee gwih-dah

Wallet	Portafoglio
Did you find your **wallet**?	Hai trovato il tuo **portafoglio**?

Porh-tah-foh-lihoh

Are you ready to create your own list? How many of those things are there in your house? Ok, let us take an example to understand it better.

Nancy: *Honey! Do you have everything you need for camp?*

Tesoro! Hai preso tutto quello che ti serve per il campeggio?

Peter: *Yes, mom. I think so.*

Si, mamma. Penso di si.

Nancy: *Do you have your id and cellphone?*

Hai preso i documenti e il cellulare?

Peter: *Yes. I cannot find my toothbrush.*

Si. Ma non riesco a trovare il mio spazzolino da denti.

Nancy: *I saw it by the bathroom's mirror.*

L'ho visto nel bagno, vicino allo specchio.

Peter: *Thanks! Can I bring my laptop?*

Grazie! Posso portare il mio portatile?

Nancy: *To camp? No! Bring your wallet. You need that.*

In campeggio? No! Portati il portafoglio. Ne avrai bisogno.

Peter: *I need money, too.*

Ho anche bisogno di soldi.

Nancy: *It is on your bed.*

Sono sul tuo letto.

Peter: *Good. I also need water and a small bin.*

Perfetto. Mi servono anche acqua e un piccolo cestino.

Nancy: *A bin? Why?*

Un cestino? Perchè?

Peter: *For the food. Haven't you read the news? It's bear season.*

Per il cibo. Non hai letto le notizie? È la stagione degli orsi.

Nancy: *Really? Ok. Keep your light close to you, just in case.*

Davvero? Ok. Tieni sempre la torcia vicino a te, per sicurezza.

Peter: *Sure. Thanks, mom.*

Va bene. Grazie, mamma.

It is getting easier; I can feel it. I guarantee that if you follow the instructions and keep repeating our little lessons, you will make rapid progress and you'll be able to communicate fluently in Italian very soon. Feel free to go back to the previous chapters as many times as you like, all it takes sometimes is just a little something to jog your memory!

If you need help to count how many times you are repeating a sentence, move on to the next chapter: we are going to learn numbers next!

Chapter 6 – How far can you count?

There are many nursery rhymes that help to introduce numbers even before a child understands numbers or how to count. It was probably through one of these songs that many of us learned numbers and measurements.

That is what we will learn in this chapter. Don't worry. You won't have to do any math!

When speaking in Italian, you will often need to use and understand numbers to express time, record dates and – of course – count. So, here is a table to help you memorize them:

		Pronunciation
One	Uno	Uh-noh
Two	Due	Doo-eh
Three	Tre	Treh
Four	Quattro	Kwua-troh

Five	Cinque	Cheen-kweh
Six	Sei	Seh-ee
Seven	Sette	She-teh
Eight	Otto	Oh-toh
Nine	Nove	Noh-veh
Ten	Dieci	Diheh-cee
Eleven	Undici	Oon-dee-cee
Twelve	Dodici	Doh-dee-cee
Thirteen	Tredici	Treh-dee-cee
Fourteen	Quattordici	Kwaht-tohr-dee-cee
Fifteen	Quindici	Kween-dee-cee
Sixteen	Sedici	Seh-dee-cee

As you can see, all the numbers from one to ten are specific words, and as such, you will have to learn it by heart. From eleven to sixteen, numbers are formed from the root of the digit (i.e. "un-") followed by ten ("-dici" instead than dieci).

For numbers from seventeen to nineteen, the order is reversed: the root -dici and then the unit:

Seventeen	Diciassette	Dee-chahs-seh-teh
Eighteen	Diciotto	Dee-cho-toh
Nineteen	Diciannove	Dee-chah-noh-veh

The same goes for numbers from 21 to 29. We just take the root number (venti) and add the unit.

Twenty	Venti	Vehn-tee
Twenty-one	Ventuno	Vehn-tooh-noh
Twenty-two	Ventidue	Vehn-tee-doo-eh
Twenty-three	Ventitrè	Vehn-tee-treh
Twenty-four	Ventiquattro	Vehn-tee-kwah-troh
Twenty-five	Venticinque	Vehn-tee-cheen-kweh
Twenty-six	Ventisei	Vehn-tee-sahy

Twenty-seven	Ventisette	Vehn-tee-seh-teh
Twenty-eight	Ventotto	Vehn-toht-oh
Twenty-nine	Ventinove	Vehn-tee-noh-veh

You may have already noticed that when the ten unit ends in a vowel (like in this case "venti") and you add a unit that begins with a vowel (i.e. "uno"), the first word loses its vowel. As a consequence, "venti" and "uno" make "ventuno".

Moreover, when a number ends in -tre, you will need to add an accent: -trè.

Thirty	Trenta	Trehn-tah
Thirty-one	Trentuno	Trehn-too-noh
Thirty-two	Trentadue	Trehn-tah-doo-eh
Forty	Quaranta	Kwah-rahn-tah
Fifty	Cinquanta	Cheen-kwahn-tah
Sixty	Sessanta	Seh-sahn-tah

Seventy	Settanta	Seh-tahn-tah
Eighty	Ottanta	Oh-tahn-tah
Ninety	Novanta	Noh-vahn-tah
One hundred	Cento	Chehn-toh
One thousand	Mille	Mee-leh

You can familiarize with numbers by repeating them to yourself over and over. It also helps if you count out loud.

Let's move on to ordinal numbers. As the name suggests, they tell the "order" of things. That way, we can make ranks, prioritize, and set dates. Awesome, uh?

First	Primo	Pree-moo
Second	Secondo	Seh-kohn-doh
Third	Terzo	Terh-tzoh
Fourth	Quarto	Kwarh-toh
Fifth	Quinto	Kwihn-toh

Sixth	Sesto	Sehs-toh
Seventh	Settimo	Seh-tee-moh
Eighth	Ottavo	Oh-tah-voh
Ninth	Nono	Noh-noh
Tenth	Decimo	Deh-chee-moh

As is the case with cardinal numbers, each of the first ten ordinal numbers has a distinct form. Form eleventh onward, ordinal numbers are formed by dropping the final vowel of the number and adding the suffix -esimo:

Eleventh	Undicesimo	Oon-dee-ceh-see-moh
Twelfth	Docicesimo	Doh-dee-ceh-see-moh
Thirteenth	Tredicesimo	Treh-dee-ceh-see-moh

Fourteenth	Quattordicesimo	Kwah-torh-dee-ceh-see-moh
Fifteenth	Quindicesimo	Kween-dee-ceh-see-moh

Let's now have a look at bigger numbers and the prefixes that will help us create even higher numbers.

Twentieth	Ventesimo	Vehn-teh-see-moh
Thirtieth	Trentesimo	Tren-teh-see-moh
Fortieth	Quarantesimo	Kwah-rahn-teh-see-moh
Fiftieth	Cinquantesimo	Cheen-kwahn-teh-see-moh
Sixtieth	Sessantesimo	Seh-sahn-teh-see-moh
Seventieth	Settantesimo	Seh-tahn-teh-see-moh

Eightieth	Ottantesimo	Oh-than-teh-see-moh
Ninetieth	Novantesimo	Noh-vahn-teh-see-moh
Hundredth	Centesimo	Chen-teh-see-moh
Thousandth	Millesimo	Mih-leh-see-moh

Now it's your turn? Try to cover the right side of the page. Can you work out the answers to the below?

21th	Ventunesimo
32th	Trentaduesimo
45th	Quarantacinquesimo
58th	Cinquattotesimo
64th	Sessantaquattresimo
79th	Settantanovesimo
83th	Ottantatreesimo
95th	Novantacinquesimo

108th	Centoottesimo

Have you seen how easy it is to create higher ordinal numbers? I know it's not a competition, but why not try to get there first?

Chapter 7 – What did you want to be when you grew up?

What did you want to be when you grew up?" How many times did someone ask you this question when you were a child? And how many times have you changed your answer?

When I was little, I wanted to be a scientist. Later on, I wanted to be a singer. Nowadays, I am a writer, but previously I have had different jobs. I have been a teacher, an electrician – honestly, not a very good one- and a chef.

We always need to remember that all professions are important. We need farmers to produce food of the highest quality, doctors to treat injuries and disease, artists to represent the beauty of the world around us, and so on.

Speaking of artists, this is a good word to start with.

Artist	Artista
Picasso was an **artist.**	Picasso era un **artista.**

Arh-tees-tah

You should always keep in mind that vowels like "a" are very open and clear in Italian. "A" is pronounced like the English word "ah!". "Artista"

Chef	Cuoco
I want to become a **chef**.	Voglio fare il **cuoco.**

Kwoh-coh

Construction worker	Muratore
My dad is a **construction worker**.	Mio papà è un **muratore**.

Mooh-rah-toh-reh

Firefighter	Pompiere
Being a **firefighter** is a risky job.	Fare il **pompiere** è un lavoro pericoloso.

Pom-peeh-eh-reh

Doctor	Dottore
The **doctor** will see you in 5 minutes.	Il **dottore** ti riceverà in 5 minuti.

Doh-toh-reh

Policeman	Poliziotto
A **policeman** came to our house.	Un **poliziotto** è venuto a casa nostra.

Poh-lee-tziho-toh

Teacher	Insegnante
That is my **teacher**.	Lei è la mia **insegnante**.

Ihn-seh-nyahn-teh

Actor/Actress	Attore/Attrice
Emma Stone is an **actress**.	Emma Stone è un'**attrice**.

Ah-toh-reh/Ah-tree-ceh

Banker	Banchiere
I am waiting for a **banker**.	Sto aspettando un **banchiere.**

Bahn-kee-eh-reh

Butcher	Macellaio

| I am calling the **butcher** to order. | Sto chiamando il **macellaio** per ordinare. |

Mah-cheh-lah-yoh

| Dentist | Dentista |
| I have a great **dentist.** | Ho un **dentista** molto bravo**.** |

Dehn-tees-tah

| Driver | Conducente |
| My **driver** is very fast. | Il mio **conducente** va molto veloce. |

Kon-doo-chen- teh

Are you making any progress?

| Electrician | Elettricista |
| You need to call the **electrician**. | Devo chiamare l'**elettricista**. |

Eh-leh-tree-cis-tah

Farmer	Contadino
My grandpa was a **farmer**.	Mio nonno faceva il **contadino**.

Kon-tah-dee-noh

Hairdresser	Parrucchiere
I have a great **hairdresser**.	Ho un bravo **parrucchiere**.

Pah-rooh-kihe-reh

Journalist	Giornalista
I will be a **journalist**.	Io farò il **giornalista**.

Jorh-nah-lihs-tah

Lawyer	Avvocato
My daughter is a **lawyer**.	Mia figlia è **avvocato**.

Ah-voh-kah-toh

Painter	Pittore
That **painter** did a good job.	Quel **pittore** ha fatto un buon lavoro.

Pee-toh-reh

www.LearnLikeNatives.com

There are plenty of professions but don't worry, we won't go through them all. Just few more words.

Politician	Politico
I want to be a **politician**.	Voglio diventare un **politico**.

Poh-lih-tee-coh

Psychologist	Psicologo
I am a **psychologist**.	Io sono **psicologo**.

Psi-koh-loh-go

Scientist	Scienziato
Scientists are addressing climate change.	Gli **scienziati** stanno affrontando il cambiamento climatico.

She-hen-tzah-toh

What did you want to be when you grew up? Let's learn few more words.

Plumber	Idraulico

| I have to call the **plumber**. | Devo chiamare l'**idraulico**. |

Ee-drau-lee-coh

Secretary	Segretaria
My **secretary** is on vacation.	La mia **segretaria** è in vacanza.

Seh-greh-tah-ree-ah

Shoemaker	Calzolaio
The **shoemaker** made a good job.	Il **calzolaio** ha fatto un buon lavoro.

Kal-zoh-lah-joh

Singer	Cantante
She's a great **singer**.	Lei è una brava **cantante**.

Kan-tan-teh

Waiter/Waitress	Cameriere/Cameriera
I'll call the **waiter**.	Chiamo il **cameriere**.

Ka-meh-riheh-reh/Ka-meh-riheh-rah

Writer	Scrittore
It is hard to be a **writer**.	È difficile diventare uno **scrittore**.

Skriht-toh-reh

Translator	Traduttore
I work as a **translator**.	Io lavoro come **traduttore**.

Tra-doo-toh-reh

Ready for a short dialogue?

Cris: *Hey! What do you have there?*

Ehi! Che cos'hai lì?

Layla: *It's a firefighter costume.*

È un costume da pompiere.

Cris: *Is November yet?*

È già Novembre?

Layla: No! My son's school is going to have a "career day".

No! La scuola di mio figlio sta organizzando una "giornata delle professioni".

Cris: Oh, I see. I wanted to be a psychologist when I was nine.

Oh, capisco. Io sognavo di diventare psicologo quando avevo nove anni.

Layla: I wanted to be a teacher. We are always changing, right?

Io volevo fare l'insegnante. Come cambiano le cose, vero?

Cris: Yeah. I also wanted to be a teacher when I was fourteen.

Si. Anche io volevo diventare professoresse quando avevo quattordici anni.

Layla: How did you decide to become a lawyer?

Poi come hai deciso di fare l'avvocato?

Cris: Well... you know. I was seventeen and wanted to change the world.

Beh... vedi. Avevo diciassette anni e volevo cambiare il mondo.

Layla: *My son wants to be a farmer.*

Mio figlio vuole fare il contadino.

Cris: *Isn't his dad a politician?*

Suo papà non fa il politico?

Layla: *Yeah. He started as a journalist and then changed careers.*

Si. Aveva iniziato come giornalista e poi ha cambiato carrierra.

Cris: *Indeed. We are always changing.*

È proprio vero. Cambiamo continuamente.

Now, repeat with me: "I wanted to be" -"Io volevo essere" and complete the sentence.

One of the first questions people ask to someone they have just meet is "What is your job?" which translates to "Che lavoro fai?". Thanks to what we have just learned in this unit, you are going to be ready for this conversation!

What next? Let's go to learn how to ask for directions.

Chapter 8 – Where are we going?

Being able to clearly tell where you want to go is very important, especially when traveling in another country. For this reason, the ability to communicate in simple situations such as asking for directions can make your life easier, in case of a SatNav failure or during a relaxing afternoon walk when you don't have your mobile with you.

Street	Strada
That is the main **street**.	Quella è la **strada** principale.

Strah-dah

Avenue	Viale
This is Liberazione **Avenue**.	Questo è il **Viale** della Liberazione.

Vihah-leh

Block	Quartiere/Isolato
We are going to the **block** party.	Stiamo andando alla festa di **quartiere**.

Kwuar-teeheh-reh / Ee-zoh-lah

Square	Piazza
The **square** should be a few blocks ahead.	La **piazza** dovrebbe essere qualche isolato più avanti.

Pihah-tzah

Are you pronouncing those vowels properly? Open vowels, remember?!

Building	Edificio
This **building** has 110 floors.	Questo **edificio** ha 110 piani.

Eh-dee-fee-choh

Monument	Monumento
This **monument** is 300 years old.	Questo **monumento** ha 300 anni.

Moh-nooh-mehn-toh

Hospital	Ospedale
The **hospital** is 5 minutes away.	L'**ospedale** dista 5 minuti da qui.

Ohs-peh-dah-leh

Corner	Angolo
The store is passing that **corner.**	Il negozio è dopo quell'**angolo**.

Ahn-goh-loh

Nearest	Più vicino
That is the **nearest** mall.	Quello è il centro commerciale **più vicino**.

Pihyou vih-chih-noh

Turn left	Girare a sinistra
You should **turn left** in two blocks.	Devi **girare a sinistra** tra due isolati.

Jih-rah-reh ah see-nihs-trah

Turn right	Girare a destra

Let's **turn right** after this corner.	Dobbiamo **girare a destra** dopo l'angolo.

Jih-rah-reh ah dehs-trah

Go straight on	Continuare dritto
You only have to **go straight** on, and you will get there.	Ti basterà **continuare dritto** e ci arriverai.

Kon-tee-noohah-reh dree-toh

Go past	Oltrepassare
You have to **go past** the main street.	Devi **oltrepassare** la strada principale.

Ohl treh-pah-sah-reh

Crossroads	Incrocio
Take a left on the **crossroads.**	Svolta a sinistra all'**incrocio**.

Ihn-croh-choh

Those phrases will take you wherever you desire! Are you ready to put into practice what we have just learned about directions?

John:	*¡Hey, sir! Good afternoon.*
	Salve, signore! Buon pomeriggio.
Vendor (Negoziante):	*What can I do for you?*
	Come posso aiutarti?
John:	*Can you tell me how I can get to the train station?*
	Puoi dirmi come raggiungere la stazione dei treni?
Vendor	*Sure. You have to go in that direction for three blocks.*
	Certo. Devi proseguire in quella direzione per tre isolati.
John:	*I have to go past the library?*
	Devo oltrepassare la biblioteca?
Vendor	*Yes. Then, you turn left and go for another five or six blocks.*
	Si. Poi, svolta a sinistra e prosegui per altri cinque o sei isolati.

John: Oh, I think I come from there. But I got confused at the crossroads.

Oh, credo di essere venuto da quella direzione. Ma ho fatto confusione all'incrocio.

Vendor Very usual. You have to take a left in the crossroads.

Succede spesso. Devi girare a sinistra all'incrocio.

John: Ok.

Va bene.

Vendor You will see a square. The station is in front.

Poi vedrai una piazza. La stazione è lì di fronte.

John: Thank you very much.

Grazie mille.

Vendor: Don't worry. Have a nice trip.

Non c'è problema. Buon viaggio.

Are you ready to go and explore a new place? Better hurry! "Survival 101" is coming.

Chapter 9 – Survival 101

Each chapter contains helpful information, but this is particularly important. We have already said that: sometimes things go wrong. Your child may feel unwell, you could twist an ankle while hiking, lose your passport…. things do happen. So it's better to be prepared, right?

I believe that this sentence, in particular, is fundamental for you:

| Do you speak English? | Parli inglese? |

Parh-lee een-gleh-she

It is a question you should always remember, as could make your life much easier.

| Where is the bathroom? | Dove posso trovare il bagno? |

Doh-veh poh-soh troh-vah-reh eel bah-nyoh

| How can I get to this place? | Come posso andare in questo posto? |

Koh-meh poh-soh ahn-dah-reh ihn kwehs-toh pohs-toh

| Where is the nearest hospital? | Dove si trova l'ospedale più vicino? |

Doh-veh see troh-vah l ohs-peh-dah-leh pihyou vih-chih-noh

Extremely important: "Dove si trova l'ospedale più vicino?".

| When is the next flight? | Quando è il prossimo volo? |

Kwuan-doh eh eel proh-sih-moh voh-loh

| Who can I talk to about this problem? | Con chi posso parlare di questo problema? |

Kon kee poh-soh parh-lah-reh dee kwehs-toh proh-bleh-mah

| Where can I find a policeman? | Dove posso trovare un agente di polizia? |

Doh-veh poh-soh troh-vah-reh uhn ahjehn-the dee poh-lih-tzih-ah

Though I hope you will never need this:

| Where is the embassy? | Dove si trova l'ambasciata? |

Doh-veh see troh-vah l ahm-bah-sciah-tah

www.LearnLikeNatives.com

| What do I need to visit…? | Cosa mi serve per visitare…? |

Koh-sah mee sehr-veh pehr vee-she-tah-reh

| Where can I find…? | Dove posso trovare …? |

Doh-veh poh-soh troh-vah-reh …

Oh, I really hope you won't need any of them. But better safe than sorry! Let's see a short dialogue now.

Harry: *Hello, sir. How can I get to Pizzeria Pino, in Due Giugno Avenue?*

Salve, signore. Come posso arrivare a Pizzeria Pino, in Viale Due Giugno?

Driver: *I can take you, but is far. Is someone waiting for you? It's rush hour.*

Posso portarti, ma è lontano. C'è qualcuno che ti aspetta? È l'ora di punta.

Harry: *No. I think I left my passport there.*

No. Credo di aver dimenticato lì il mio passaporto.

Driver: *It will take us at least 40 minutes to get there.*

Ci metteremo almeno 40 minuti per arrivarci.

Harry: *Ok. Maybe I can call someone there.*

Va bene. Magari posso telefonare.

Vendor: *Good afternoon. Pizzeria Pino.*

Buon pomeriggio. Pizzeria Pino.

Harry: *Hello! My name is Harry Klein. I was there last night, and I think I left my passport.*

Salve! Mi chiamo Harry Klein. Ero lì ieri sera, e penso di aver dimenticato il mio passaporto.

Vendor: *One second, please. Do you remember where you were sitting?*

Un attimo, per favore. Ti ricordi dove stavi seduto?

Harry: *Yes. I was at the bar, by the corner.*

Si. Ero al bar, all'angolo.

Vendor: *Ok. Give me a second.*

Va bene. Dammi un momento.

Harry: Ok.

Ok.

Vendor: *Yeah. I just consulted my coworkers, and they did not find anything. I am sorry.*

Allora. Ho appena parlato con i miei colleghi e non hanno trovato nulla. Mi dispiace.

Harry: *Thank you.*

Grazie.

Driver: *They didn't find it?*

Non lo hanno trovato?

Harry: *No. Where is the nearest police station?*

No. Dov'è la stazione di polizia più vicina?

Driver: *Don't you want to go to your embassy? It could be better.*

Non vuoi andare alla tua ambasciata? Sarebbe meglio.

Harry: *Oh, yes. Where's the UK embassy?*

Oh, giusto. Dov'è l'ambasciata del Regno Unito?

Driver: Actually, it is near from here. We will be there in a few minutes.

È proprio qui vicino. Saremo lì in pochi minuti.

What a nightmare to lose your passport abroad! I sincerely hope you will never have to use any of these phrases.

Now, let's move on to something less stressful. Shall we switch to colors?

Chapter 10 – What is the color of the sky?

I will tell you a secret: I love a wonderful view, and everywhere I go, I like to just lose myself gazing at the sky. I particularly love the sunset. I also like the sunrise, but I'm really not a morning person.

How many colors are there in the sky?

Yellow	Giallo / Gialla
My dress is **yellow**.	Il mio vestito è **giallo**.

Jahl-loh / Jahl-loh

Blue	Blu
The sky looks very **blue**.	Il cielo è **blu**.

Bloo

Red	Rosso / Rossa
I bought a **red** car.	Ho comprato un'auto **rossa**.

Rho-soh / Rho-sah

Purple	Viola
Those flowers are **purple**.	Quei fiori sono **viola**.

Vihoh-lah

Pink	Rosa
My daughter wants a **pink** gown.	Mia figlia vuole una vestaglia **rosa**.

Roh-sah

Green	Verde
The fields look very **green** this year.	I campi sono molto **verdi** quest'anno.

Verh-deh

Orange	Arancione
I want an **orange** t-shirt.	Voglio una maglietta **arancione**.

Ah-rahn-choh-neh

Brown	Marrone

| Your dog is **brown**. | Il tuo cane è **marrone**. |

Mah-roh-neh

Grey	Grigio
Grey is a mixed color.	Il **grigio** è un colore misto.

Grih-joh

Black	Nero
Black is my favorite color.	Il **nero** è il mio colore preferito.

Neh-roh

White	Bianco
I painted the walls **white**.	Ho dipinto le pareti di **bianco**.

Bee-ahn-coh

Fun fact: black and white are not colors. They represent, respectively, the absence of light and the lack of shadow.

Let's look at an example.

Lisa: *Hey, honey! I need your help with something.*

Ehi, dolcezza. Ho bisogno del tuo aiuto con una cosa.

Alex: *Yes, love. What is it?*

Certo, amore. Di che si tratta?

Lisa: *We need to pick the colors for the house before we move.*

Prima di trasferirci dobbiamo scegliere i colori per la casa.

Alex: *Oh, true. What do you have in mind?*

Oh, certo. Cosa avevi in mente?

Lisa: *I was thinking of a light blue for our room, with touches of yellow.*

Stavo pensando ad un blu chiaro per la nostra camera, con tocchi di giallo.

Alex: *Ok. What have you thought of the living room?*

Va bene. E che idee hai per la sala?

Lisa: *I am thinking of a combination of red and white walls.*

Sto pensando a una combinazione di pareti rosse e bianche.

Alex: *Do you think that my black chair will match?*

Pensi andrà bene con la mia poltrona nera?

Lisa: *Positive. And for the studio, I was looking for something more neutral.*

Certamente. E per lo studio, vorrei qualcosa di più neutro.

Alex: *By neutral you mean...?*

Cosa intendi per neutro...?

Lisa: *Earth colors. Like a light brown.*

Colori della terra. Come marrone chiaro.

Alex: *And the nursery?*

E per la cameretta?

Lisa: *Grey, with a purple wall.*

Grigio, con una parete viola.

Alex: *It sounds amazing. Thanks for planning all this.*

Sembra perfetto. Grazie per aver pianificato tutto.

Lisa: *Sure! I love it!*

Certo! Mi fa piacere!

What about you? Are you already planning to repaint your whole house? And for your dining room, would you like to go and buy some lanterns at an artisanal market in Venice? Imagine all the things you could do! First of all, however, we need to get there. Shall we do that?

Chapter 11 – So much to do, so much to see

Where do you dream of going? Personally, I love the mountains. I grew up in a village in the valley, with a stunning view of the mountains. I think maybe that's why I do love mountains so much! But anyway, enough about me. Now, imagine where you would like to go.

Travel	Viaggiare
She lost the scarf during her last **travel**.	Ha perso la sua sciarpa durante il suo ultimo **viaggio**.

Vihah-jah-reh

Ticket	Biglietto
I bought a two-way **ticket**.	Ho comprato un **biglietto** andata e ritorno.

Bee-liheh-toh

Airplane	Aereo

| This **airplane** is very big. | Questo **aereo** è molto grande. |

Ah-eh-rih-oh

| Reservation | Prenotazione |
| He made a **reservation** for tonight. | Lui ha una **prenotazione** per questa notte. |

Preh-noh-taht-zihoh-neh

| Hotel | Hotel |
| I like this **hotel**. | Mi piace questo **hotel**. |

Oh-tehl

| Room | Camera |
| They need a double **room**. | Loro vogliono una **camera** doppia. |

Cah-meh-rah

| Key | Chiave |
| I lost my **key**. | Ho perso la **chiave**. |

Kihah-veh

Passport	Passaporto
Can I see your **passport**?	Posso vedere il tuo **passaporto**?

Pah-sah-porh-toh

Taxi	Taxi
Let's take a **taxi.**	Prendiamo un **taxi**.

Tax-see

"Taxi" is the same both in Italian and in English.

Car rental	Noleggio auto
Where is the **car rental**?	Dove si trova il **noleggio auto?**

Noh-leh-joh how-toh

Bus	Autobus
We will take the **bus.**	Noi prenderemo l'**autobus**.

How-toh-boohs

Subway	Metropolitana

| The subway was out of service. | La **metropolitana** è fuori servizio. |

Meh-troh-poh-lih-tah-nah

| Train | Treno |
| I'll take the **train**. | Io prenderò il **treno**. |

Treh-noh

| Station | Stazione |
| That is the nearest **station**. | Quella è la **stazione** più vicina. |

Stah-tzioh-neh

| Theater | Teatro |
| This **theater** was remodeled 5 years ago. | Questo **teatro** è stato ristrutturato 5 anni fa. |

Teh-ah-troh

| Beach | Spiaggia |
| She wants to go to the **beach**. | Lei vuole andare in **spiaggia**. |

Spihah-jah

www.LearnLikeNatives.com

Mountain	Montagna
They want to climb that **mountain.**	Loro vogliono scalare quella **montagna.**

Mohn-tah-nyah

Island	Isola
Let's go to that **island**.	Andiamo su quell'**isola**.

Ee-zoh-lah

City	Città
Milan is a very big **city**.	Milano è una **città** molto grande.

Chih-tah

Are you ready? You know what's coming next!

Shaun: *I want to buy the tickets for our travel. Can we decide on something?*

Voglio comprare i biglietti per il nostro viaggio. Possiamo decidere qualcosa?

Vanessa: *Sure! Where do we want to go?*

Certo! Dove vogliamo andare?

Shaun: *Not another city. I want to rest.*

Nessun altra città. Voglio riposarmi.

Vanessa: *I agree. Do you remember that beautiful mountain that Lisa showed us? Cortina D'Ampezzo.*

Sono d'accordo. Ti ricordi quel bel posto di montagna che ci ha mostrato Lisa? Cortina D'Ampezzo.

Shaun: *Oh, sure. That cozy mountain house, right?*

Oh, certo. Quella casa di montagna tanto carina, giusto?

Vanessa: *Yes. That one.*

Si. Proprio quella.

Shaun: *That sounds great. Do you think it is available?*

Che bella idea. Pensi abbiamo disponibilità?

Vanessa: *On it!*

Ci guardo!

Shaun: *Remember to check for a view.*

Cerca di trovare qualcosa con una bella vista.

Vanessa: *I got the perfect room! It is beautiful.*

Ho trovato la stanza perfetta. È carinissima.

Shaun: *Great. I need our passports to buy the tickets. I'll get them.*

Fantastico. Ho bisogno dei passaporti per comprare i biglietti. Li prenderò io.

Vanessa: *Sure. I am excited!*

Perfetto. Non vedo l'ora!

So, are you getting excited?

Repeat with me: "voglio andare a" –I want to travel to-, and make it happen. Traveling is an amazing way to meet new people and discover beautiful places. In my opinion, traveling is growing up and you can never end it!

A spontaneous trip, a last-second vacation… these are usually the best things, the kind of stories you will remember forever. Some memories are just amazing!

And do you know what else I like when traveling? The food!

www.LearnLikeNatives.com

A Quick Message

Before we start the final chapter of this book.

"No one can whistle a symphony. It takes a whole orchestra to play it." –

H.E. Luccock

Do you want to be part of the orchestra of the Learning Italian community?

Here is how:

If you're enjoying this book, I would like to kindly ask you to leave a brief review on Amazon.

Reviews aren't easy to come by, but they have a profound impact in supporting my work. This way, I can keep creating new content to help the whole community at my very best.

www.LearnLikeNatives.com

I would be incredibly thankful if you could just take a minute to leave a quick review on Amazon, even if it's just a sentence or two!

It's that simple!

Thank you so much for taking the time to leave a short review on Amazon.

The community and I are very appreciative, as your review makes a difference.

Now, let's get back to learning Italian!

Chapter 12 – I am a bit hungry

Food is a language that everyone understands. Food talks about us, about culture, and lifestyle. If you visit a foreign country, you have to at least try the local cuisine.

If you ask my opinion, I strongly believe that Italy has given the world one of its great cuisines: there is nothing like that! It is viewed as a form of art by many. However, contrary to common belief, there is no such a thing as "Italian cuisine", as this it is in reality a collection of different regional cuisines. You should know that Italians are deeply proud of their food. Even UNESCO has recognized the Mediterranean Diet (using fresh tomatoes, olive oil, and garlic) on a list of "Intangible Cultural Heritage of Humanity".

In the past centuries, a lot of Italians have emigrated, mainly to America, taking with them their culinary experience. Of course, coming in contact with different cultures widens their view and obliged them to make some changes to the original recipes.

www.LearnLikeNatives.com

I am sure that local people will love to tell you everything about their cuisine, but for now, let me just teach you a few basics words.

Let's start with breakfast.

Cappuccino	Cappuccino
A **cappuccino,** please.	Un **cappuccino** per favore.

Kah-pooh-cee-noh

I'm sure you are already familiar with this word. It is usually a breakfast drink, and no Italian would have one after 11am or with a meal.

Milk	Latte
I think this **milk** has gone bad.	Credo il **latte** sia andato a male.

Lah-the

Contrary to what happens in England, if you ask for a "latte" in Italy, you would be presented with a glass of milk. So be sure to use its full name: "Caffelatte" – literally coffee with milk.

Croissant	Cornetto
Breakfast includes **croissant** and cappuccino.	La colazione è **cornetto** e cappuccino.

Kohr-neh-toh

If you wish to sound like an Italian native, in the morning, you should go to the bar and ask for "cornetto e cappuccino". This is the typical Italian breakfast, a sweet treat.

Cake	Torta
Have another slice of **cake**.	Prendi un'altra fetta di **torta**.

Torh-tah

Pancakes	Frittelle
These **pancakes** are fluffy.	Queste **frittelle** sono soffici.

Free-the-leh

Hope you are getting hungry because it's time to go to a pizzeria:

Pizza	Pizza
We are going out for a **pizza** tonight.	Usciamo a mangiare la **pizza** stasera.

Peeh-tzah

Tomato	Pomodoro
You only need a few **tomatoes**.	Ti serve solo qualche pomodoro.

Poh-moh-dorh-roh

Basil	Basilico
I have a **basil** plant.	Ho una pianta di **basilico.**

Bah-zee-lee-koh

Do you know the story of the most popular pizza margherita? In 1889, an Italian chef created a dish for Queen Margherita. It was a dough base with tomatoes, mozzarella cheese and fresh basil. The ingredients were resembling the Italian flag.

As the years passed, many variations of this pizza started to become available, but be careful when you order a pizza in Italy. Ordering a Hawaiian pizza would be a great mistake! Italians are purist when it comes to food, and pineapple does not belong on pizza.

Pepperoni pizza	Pizza con il salame
I would like a **pepperoni pizza**.	Vorrei una **pizza** con il salame.

Peeh-tzah kohn eel sah-lah-meh

Peppers	Peperoni
I've bought **peppers** and potatoes.	Ho comprato **peperoni** e patate.

Peh-peh-roh-nee

Yes, you have got it right! I am sure you love pepperoni pizza, but if you ask for it in Italy, they will serve you a pizza with… peppers! If you want a pepperoni, you should order a "pizza con salame" or "diavola".

Pasta	Pasta
Italians eat a lot of **pasta.**	Gli Italiani mangiano un sacco di **pasta**.

Pah-stah

Pasta is an important part of the Italian cuisine. It comes in a wide range of shapes and lengths. The most popular are probably spaghetti, fusilli and:

Lasagna	Lasagna
Lasagna is my favorite food.	Il cibo che preferisco è la **lasagna**.

Lah-sah-nah

Meatballs	Poplette
We had **meatballs** for dinner.	Abbiamo mangiato **polpette** per cena.

Pohl-peh-teh

Now, this is probably the biggest Italian myth: In Italy, you will not find a dish called "spaghetti and meatballs". This is an American creation, and not an authentic Italian dish.

Similarly, the Bolognese sauce is most common in the US as in Italy, this only refers to the one produced in Bologna, while every region has its own kind of sauce. The proper name of this minced meat in tomato sauce is "ragù" (rah-gooh).

Also, Italians do not eat pasta with chicken.

Egg	Uova
She wants **eggs** and ham.	Lei vuole **uova** e prosciutto.

Woh-vah

Cheese	Formaggio
I don't eat **cheese**.	Io non mangio **formaggio**.

Forh-mah-joh

Butter	Burro
French people love **butter.**	I Francesi amano il **burro**.

Booh-roh

Sandwich	Panino
We want five **sandwiches**.	Vogliamo cinque **panini**.

Pah-nee-noh

Does it sound familiar? I am sure you have ordered a "panini" before. You should be aware that "panini" is plural and means sandwiches. If you only want one sandwich, make sure to order a "panino".

Salad	Insalata
I want a Caprese **salad.**	Io vorrei un'**insalata** Caprese.

Ihn-sah-lah-tah

Sausage	Salsiccia
We love **sausages** for breakfast.	A noi piace mangiare **salsiccia** a colazione.

Sal-sih-chah

Bread	Pane
I bought the **bread** this morning.	Ho comprato il **pane** questa mattina.

Pah-neh

Artisanal bread is a big thing in Italy, and if you enter a local bakery, you will find plenty of different types of bread. Very popular is also "bruschetta" (Brews-keh-tah): a cooked slice of bread topped with chopped tomatoes.

Ham	Prosciutto
The flavor of **ham** is delicious.	Il sapore del **prosciutto** è delizioso.

Proh-shoo-toh

Chicken	Pollo
That **chicken** is raw.	Quel **pollo** è crudo.

Poh-loh

Rice	Riso
The **rice** is ready.	Il **riso** è pronto.

Ree-zoh

Soup	Zuppa
This **soup** is hot.	Questa **zuppa** è calda.

Zooh-pah

Onion	Cipolla
I was chopping **onions**.	Stavo tagliando le **cipolle**.

Chih-poh-lah

Garlic	Aglio
You need to add **garlic** and stir.	Devi aggiungere **aglio** e mescolare.

Ah-lih-oh

Lemon	Limone
These **lemons** look very nice.	Questi **limoni** sembrano molto buoni.

Lee-moh-neh

Orange	Arancia
I would like an **orange** juice, please.	Vorrei un succo di **arancia**, per favore.

Ah-rahn-chah

Peanut	Arachidi

| I am allergic to **peanuts**. | Sono allergico agli **arachidi**. |

Ah-rah-kee-dee

"Arachidi" is an important one. It is, after all, one of the most common food allergies.

We are almost done with this first level!

Just one more conversation! Let's go!

Veronica: *I am hungry.*

Ho fame.

Karol: *Let's see. If you fancy something sweet, there are still some croissants from the breakfast.*

Vediamo. Se hai voglia di qualcosa di dolce, ci sono ancora dei cornetti dalla colazione.

Veronica: *Uhm... Not really. Do we have ham and cheese? I could use the bread to prepare a panini.*

Uhm... Non proprio. Abbiamo prosciutto e formaggio? Potrei usare il pane per preparare un panino.

Karol: *No. I could not go grocery shopping yesterday.*

No. Non sono andata a fare la spesa ieri.

Veronica: *It is fine. Maybe I could go to that pizza place, by the corner.*

Non c'è problema. Magari potrei andare a quel posto che fa la pizza, all'angolo.

Karol: *I don't think it is open yet.*

Non penso sia ancora aperto.

Veronica: *Oh... I will go to buy some chicken, then. Do you want anything?*

Oh... allora, vado a comprare del pollo. Ti serve altro?

Karol: *That sounds nice! Can you get me a salad?*

Buona idea! Puoi prendermi un'insalata?

Veronica: *Sure! What kind of salad would you like?*

www.LearnLikeNatives.com

Certo! Che tipo di insalata vuoi?

Karol: *Maybe a chicken Caprese salad.*

Magari una insalata caprese.

Veronica: *Sounds fine. I will come back soon.*

Va bene. Tornerò presto.

I hope it wasn't too difficult as food is very important. Do you agree?

Conclusion

Congratulations, you've made it! See, it wasn't too hard, was it?

As you realized by now, this wasn't a typical language book. If you tried and failed to learn Italian in the past, you now discovered a new approach, one that you can build on to take your Italian adventure to the next level. In going away from formal vocabulary and grammar lessons, together we shifted your focus from 'learning' Italian, to 'speaking' Italian. Two very different things!

More than just the "rules" of Italian grammar, today you have a sense of "the soul and music" of the Italian language. You built a truly solid foundation in Italian and, even if you don't realize it yet, you are now capable of navigating social situations, create connections, keep contacts, as well as make friends. As I mentioned at the start, what's the point in knowing grammatical rules if you can't order your own food!

I won't bore you with the reasons why being able to speak another language is a huge benefit for you. Or why Italian in particular will open a world of opportunities. I'm sure you're already convinced! But learning a new language is indeed a complex and rich experience, making this book a journey – your journey – into a new culture.

A beautiful culture you're now part of.

No one is ever 'ready', so get out there! Travel, read fiction and newspapers in Italian, watch films, eat Italian foods, make Italian friends, and immerse yourself in Italian-speaking culture. Sure, you'll make a few mistakes at first. But who cares! You can always go back through our lessons and keep building your confidence. I'm sure you'll get there in no time.

This is just the first volume of this series, all packed full of vocabulary and dialogs, covering essential, everyday Italian that will ensure you master the basics.

www.LearnLikeNatives.com

You can find the rest of the books in the series, as well as a whole host of other resources, at **LearnLikeNatives.com**. Simply add the book to your library to take the next step in your language learning journey. If you are ever in need of new ideas or direction, refer to our 'Speak Like a Native' eBook, available to you for free at **LearnLikeNatives.com**, which clearly outlines practical steps you can take to continue learning any language you choose.

A language should be lived, not just learned. So learn it, live it and, most importantly, enjoy it!

www.LearnLikeNatives.com

www.LearnLikeNatives.com

Learn Like a Native is a revolutionary **language education brand** that is taking the linguistic world by storm. Forget boring grammar books that never get you anywhere, Learn Like a Native teaches you languages in a fast and fun way that actually works!

As an international, multichannel, language learning platform, we provide **books, audio guides and eBooks** so that you can acquire the knowledge you need, swiftly and easily.

Our **subject-based learning**, structured around real-world scenarios, builds your conversational muscle and ensures you learn the content most relevant to your requirements.
Discover our tools at ***LearnLikeNatives.com***

When it comes to learning languages, we've got you covered!

www.LearnLikeNatives.com

www.LearnLikeNatives.com

FREE BOOK!

Get the *FREE BOOK* that reveals the secrets path to learn any language fast, and without leaving your country.

Discover:

- The **language 5 golden rules** to master languages at will

- Proven **mind training techniques** to revolutionize your learning

- A complete step-by-step guide to **conquering any language**

www.LearnLikeNatives.com

www.LearnLikeNatives.com

www.LearnLikeNatives.com

Learn Italian Like a Native *for Beginners - Level 2*

Learning Italian in Your Car Has Never Been Easier! Have Fun with Crazy Vocabulary, Daily Used Phrases, Exercises & Correct Pronunciations

www.LearnLikeNatives.com

www.LearnLikeNatives.com

www.LearnLikeNatives.com

Chapter 1 – Dreaming of the South

You are relaxing at home, dreaming of the perfect vacation, when you receive a call from a good friend who wants to tell you about his recent family holiday to South Italy--it was an amazing and diverse place, which combines art, heritage, and sunny weather. When you get off the phone, you start to imagine yourself with a glass of wine in hand, sitting in a little historical square.

Can you imagine getting lost with your family in the narrow streets of Venice? Can you hear the laughter of your loved ones, while you all enjoy a meat and cheese board at sunset? What if you could have it all?

To make this a reality, you will need to find out what are the requirements of the country you wish to visit, book flights and find an hotel.

English	Italian
To travel	Viaggiare
I love **to travel**.	Io amo **viaggiare**.

Vee-ah-jah-reh

Entry requirements	Requisiti d'ingresso
Requirements to travel to Italy.	**Requisiti d'ingresso** per viaggiare in Italia.

Reh-kwee-see-tee dee een-greh-soh

Reproduce the sound of the Italian "r" is usually quite "difficult" for English speakers. Italian has two different sounds: one for the "single r," and one for the "double r". We will not be too strict about this because it takes practice. In any case, this is what I would recommend to improve your pronunciation:

1. Lift your tongue to touch the hard palate. This is the space situated just behind your incisive upper teeth.

2. Breathe in and out through your mouth. This should make your tongue vibrate a little bit.

3. Repeat.

4. You can practice this until your "r" sounds like a purring kitten. Once you achieved this, your pronunciation will be perfect.

Let's go back to the entry requirements--checking this is very important. In some countries, due to political situations or health conditions, you may need something else, like a travel visa.

Visa	Visa
Do I need a **visa** to travel to Italy?	Ho bisogno di un **visto** per andare in Italia?

Once you have sorted all the necessary documentation, the next step would be to book your flights.

Most airline websites are now multilingual. However, it is common knowledge that internal flights are usually cheaper when purchased with a national airline.

Airlines	Compagnie aeree
What **airlines** travel to Italy?	Che **compagnie aeree** volano in Italia?

Cohm-pah-nih-ah ah-eh-reheh

You should always keep in mind that Italian vowels sound very open and clear. For example, the Italian "e" always has a similar sound to the one in "essay". That starting "e" sound is what we are looking for.

Flights	Voli
Find **flights** from Venice to Rome.	Trova **voli** da Venezia a Roma.

Voh-lee

You can notice how the word "from" translates to "da", which is your starting point. While your destination is covered by "a".

One-way ticket	Biglietto di sola andata
Do you want a **one-way trip**?	Vuole un **biglietto di sola andata**?

Bee-glee-eh-toh dee soh-lah ahn-dah-tah

Round trip	Andata e ritorno
No, I want a **round trip**.	No. Vorrei un biglietto **andata e ritorno**.

Bee-glee-eh-toh ahn-dah-tah eh ree-tohr-noh

Dates	Date
Dates for your travel?	**Date** del vostro viaggio?

Dah-the

As you can see these are two very similar words; however, the pronunciation is different. Repeat after me: Dah-teh.

When looking for accommodations, there are many options but, whether possible, it is always advisable to speak with a local to get some good tips and avoid tourist traps.

To stay	Stare
Best places **to stay** in Milan.	Posti migliori in cui **stare** a Milano.

Stah-reh

Touristic	Turistici
Most **touristic** places in Rome.	Posti più **turistici** di Roma.

www.LearnLikeNatives.com

Too-rees-tee-cee

Once you have found something you like, the next step is to book a room.

To Book	Prenotare
I want to **book** a room.	Vorrei **prenotare** una stanza.

As you can see, this is another word where you need to train your "r" pronunciation. Repeat after me: Preh-noh-tah-reh.

Good! Are we acing those r's or what?

Depending on how many people you are traveling with, you are going to need a single room or a double room.

Single room	Camera singola
I want a **single room.**	Vorrei una **camera singola**.

Cah-meh-rah seen-goh-lah

Double room	Camera doppia

I want a **double room**.	Vorrei una **camera doppia**.

Cah-meh-rah doh-pee-ah

If you are afraid of flying, I'm sure you would rather use another means of transportation.

Cruise	Crociera
I want to go on a **cruise** in the Mediterranean.	Voglio andare in **crociera** nel Mediterraneo.

Croh-cheh-rah

How do you feel, so far? Ready to leave for your next vacation?

Great! Let's pack!

First of all, you will need to know the verb that makes it possible: to pack.

To pack	Preparare
I need to **pack** my baggage.	Devo **preparare** il mio bagaglio.

Preh-pah-rah-reh

There are two very important words in this sentence: "packing" and "baggage". These translate respectively as "preparare" and "bagaglio".

With this in mind, repeat again: Devo preparare il mio bagaglio.

Of course, you will need a suitcase!

Suitcase	Valigia
I need a bigger **suitcase**.	Ho bisogno di una **valigia** più grande.

Vah-lee-jah

The word "valigia" and "bagaglio" can be used as an equivalent. Moreover, as it happens in English, there is a distinction between hand luggage and checked baggage.

Checked bag	Bagaglio da stiva
Your ticket includes one **checked bag**.	Il tuo biglietto include un **bagaglio da stiva**.

Bah-gah-glee-oh dah stee-vah

Hand luggage	Bagaglio a mano
Your **hand luggage** is too big.	Il tuo **bagaglio a mano** è troppo grande.

Bah-gah-glee-oh ah mah-noh

Now there is an open suitcase on your bed. It's time to pack!

Shirt	Camicia
This **shirt** will be perfect for the trip.	Questa **camicia** sarà perfetta per la mia vacanza.

Kah-mee-cee-ah

T-shirt	Maglietta
Why don't you bring a **t-shirt**? Something sportier.	Perchè non porti una **maglietta**? Qualcosa di più sportivo.

Mah-glee-eh-tah

Trousers	Pantaloni

| Do I have to wear long **trousers**? | Dovrò indossare **pantaloni** lunghi? |

Pahn-tah-loh-nee

Shorts	Pantaloni corti
Maybe I should pack some **shorts**.	Dovrei mettere in valigia dei **pantaloni corti**.

Pahn-tah-loh-nee kohr-tee

Due to globalization, "shorts" is a common way to call short trousers, even in Italian. But just in case, you better learn the Italian version as well: pantaloni corti or "pantaloncini".

Skirt/Dress	Gonna/Vestito
I think I will pack a **skirt** and maybe a **dress**.	Credo porterò una **gonna** e forse un **vestito**.

Skirt: Goh-nah

Dress: Vehs-tee-toh

| Jacket | Giacca |

I will bring a **jacket**.	Porterò una **giacca**.

This is a very useful one, so repeat: jah-kah. This is a general word that can work for anything in between a jacket and a raincoat. Keep it in mind: "giacca" will keep you warm if needed. If you are looking to wear something smarter, you may want to try a "coat" or "cappotto".

Underwear	Intimo
Pack **underwear** for a week.	Porta **intimo** per una settimana.

Een-tee-moh

Socks	Calzini
How many **socks** should I bring?	Quanti **calzini** porto?

Cahl-zee-nee

And, while we are on that, it is a good idea to go through some body parts.

Feet	Piedi

www.LearnLikeNatives.com

| You have very cold **feet**. | I tuoi **piedi** sono molto freddi. |

Pee-eh-dee

| Legs | Gambe |
| I have to shave my **legs**. | Devo depilarmi le **gambe**. |

Gahm-beh

| Hands | Mani |
| Do not forget the **hand** cream. | Non dimenticare la crema per le **mani**. |

Mah-nee

| Arms | Braccia |
| I want to tan my **arms**. | Voglio abbronzarmi le **braccia**. |

Brah-chah

Head	Testa
I got a bump on my **head**.	Ho un bernoccolo in **testa**.

Tehs-tah

Face	Viso
I need a **face** towel.	Mi serve un asciugamano per il **viso**.

Vee-soh

How are you doing so far? Have you seen how many words you can now add to your vocabulary?

Before moving on to a little conversation to practice our first lesson, we should briefly speak about the use of the formal form "Lei". While in English there is no difference between formal and informal, Italian has a separate form to address others in formal situations. For example, at the doctor, restaurant, when talking to the elderly or addressing strangers. In these cases and any other time you need to show respect or want to be polite, you will use "Lei".

As you will see, it is really easy to create the formal version: all you need to do is conjugate the verb at the third person singular (Lei), instead than using the second person singular (Tu). As a general rule, keep in mind that lei" could mean "she" (informal) or "you" (formal, both masculine and feminine)

To start with, we are looking at a conversation between you and a travel agent. In this example, we will use "Lei" in its formal version.

Agent: *Good afternoon! Where do you want to travel?*

Buon pomeriggio! Lei dove vorrebbe andare?

Agent: *Date for your travel?*

Date del viaggio?

Agent: *How many adults are traveling?*

Quanti adulti?

Allen: *Two, please.*

Due, per favore.

Agent: *Are you traveling with kids?*

Viaggia con bambini?

Allen: *Yes. Two kids.*

Si. Due bambini.

Agent: *Would you like a one-way trip or a round trip?*

Desidera un biglietto di sola andata o andata e ritorno?

Allen: *Round trip. Thank you.*

Andata e ritorno. Grazie.

Agent: *When do you wish to come back?*

Quando vuole ritornare?

Allen: *January, 2nd.*

Il 2 di gennaio.

Agent: *Okay. Our lowest fare is $350 per person, but it does not include checked bags. Would you like to add checked bags?*

Ok. La tariffa più bassa che possiamo offrirle è di $350 a persona, ma non include il bagaglio da stiva. Desidera aggiungerlo?

Allen: *Not at the moment. Thank you.*

No, al momento no. Grazie.

Agent: Very well. Would you like to book accommodations?

Molto bene. Vuole prenotare una sistemazione?

Allen: Sure. What do you have?

Certo. Cosa propone?

Agent: I can offer you two bedrooms. One double with a King size bed, and another double with two single beds.

Posso offrirle due camere. Una camera doppia con letto matrimoniale grande, e una stanza doppia con due letti singoli.

Allen: Great!

Fantastico!

Agent: Perfect. Please, wait in line for a second so I can write down your details.

Perfetto. Per favore, attenda un attimo in linea mentre prendo nota dei suoi dati.

How was this for you? Are you feeling more confident now? I hope you do, because we are going to the airport: we have got a plane to catch!

Chapter 2 – Not Only Birds Can Fly

I can attest from personal experience that airports are probably one of the most stressful places for several reasons. They are packed full of people with enormous queues and endless waiting times. Thankfully, I am here to help you get to your gate in time, without any stress.

Let's start by checking you in to your flight.

Passport	Passaporto
Can I please have your **passport?**	Posso vedere il suo **passaporto?**

Pah-sah-porh-toh

The check-in desk offers the ideal opportunity to practice what we learned in chapter one. They are going to ask you where you are traveling to, how many people are traveling with you, and the number of bags you wish to check-in. Unfortunately, overweight luggage is also a VERY frequent problem.

Overweight	Sovrappeso

| This piece of luggage is **overweight.** | Questo bagaglio è in **sovrappeso**. |

Come again: soh-vrah-peh-soh

If you managed to avoid the overweight charges—which I hope, as those fees are usually very high—you are ready to go through security controls.

Tray	Contenitore
Please take off shoes, coats, and metal objects, and put your belongings in the **tray** provided.	Per favore, rimuovere le scarpe, cappotti e oggetti di metallo, e riporre ogni effetto personale nell'apposito **contenitore.**

Vah-soh-yoh

Check	Controllo
Please, go to the left for a second **screen.**	Per favore, vada a sinistra per un secondo **controllo**.

Kon-troh-loh

Once past the security checks, it is time to find your gate.

Gate	Porta d'imbarco
Where is **gate** 15?	Dove si trova la **porta d'imbarco** 15?

Porh-tah dee eem-bahr-coh

Flight	Volo
What **flight** are you taking?	Che **volo** devi prendere?

Voh-loh

Boarding pass	Carta d'imbarco
Please, have your **boarding pass** and passport in hand.	Per favore, tenere pronti **carta d'imbarco** e passaporto.

This is a tricky one because it is a compound word. So, let's repeat it again.

Carh-tah dee eem-bahr-coh

Seat	Posto
My **seat** is 23F.	Il mio **posto** è il 23F.

Pohs-toh

Bathroom	Bagno
Is that **bathroom** free?	È libero il **bagno**?

Bah-nyoh

Blanket	Coperta
Can I have a **blanket**?	Posso avere una **coperta**?

Koh-perh-tah

You know, I could teach you how to ask for other things… like wine perhaps? Wine translates to "vino" – Vee-noh.

But let us be responsible and move on to learn more important things.

Go through	Passare
I need to **go through**.	Ho bisogno di **passare**.

Pah-sah-reh

Feeling sick	Stare male
I am feeling **sick.**	Mi **sento male**.

Stah-reh mah-leh

"Sick" translates to "sentirsi male" o "malato". It is a good word to remember.

Headache	Mal di testa
I have a **headache**.	Ho **mal di testa**.

Mahl dee tehs-tah

Fever	Febbre
I have a **fever**.	Ho la **febbre**.

Feh-breh

Nausea	Nausea
I feel **nauseous**.	Ho la **nausea**.

Now-seh-ah

Allergic	Allergico
I am **allergic** to…	Sono **allergico** a…

Ah-lerh-jih-coh

Obviously, I really hope you won't need to use any of these words, but it's better to be prepared for even unpleasant situations.

What are your thoughts so far? Look at everything that we have just learned. Now you will be able to speak with the airport's staff, catch a plane, enjoy a movie, and land safely. Join me for a little dialogue.

Flight Attendant: *Hello! Boarding pass, please.*

Salve! Carta d'imbarco, per favore.

Cris: *Hello!*

Salve!

Flight Attendant: *Welcome! You're at seat 14F. By the window.*

Benvenuto! Il suo posto è il 14F. Posto finestrino.

Cris:	*Thanks!*
	Grazie!
Flight Attendant:	*What would you like to drink today?*
	Cosa desidera bere?
Cris:	*I would like some water with ice.*
	Vorrei dell'acqua con ghiaccio.
Flight Attendant:	*Of course! Anything else I can do for you?*
	Certamente! Posso fare altro per Lei?
Cris:	*Yes, I am actually feeling a little sick.*
	Si. Sto iniziando a sentirmi un po' male.
Flight Attendant:	*What are your symptoms?*
	Che sintomi ha?
Cris:	*I have a headache and a slight fever.*
	Ho mal di testa e un pò di febbre.
Flight Attendant:	*Are you allergic to something?*
	È allergico a qualcosa?

Cris:	*Only to aspirin.*
	Solo all'aspirina.
Flight Attendant:	*Ok. Please wait here while I get some help.*
	Va bene. Per favore attenda mentre vado a chiedere aiuto.

Yes, I know what you are thinking. I have chosen the sick-person situation as an example. But how can you blame me? After all, I warned you that this book has been studied for you to feel confident in any situation! How is your head? Are you feeling any better? Not yet? Don't worry. We are landing now.

Chapter 3 – Do you Need a Ride?

Welcome to the holiday you have always dreamed about! There's just one more thing you will have to worry about before you can enjoy a refreshing drink in Venice's popular San Marco square: how to get to your hotel. And so, the time has come to test your knowledge. Now that you have arrived at your destination, your super-intensive-Italian immersion is about to start. How exciting is that?

First, let's begin with some basic words.

Taxi	Taxi
I need a **taxi**.	Ho bisogno di un **taxi**.

Taxi is the same in English as it is in Italian! 1 point for globalization!

Shuttle	Navetta
Where can I get a **shuttle** to the Hilton Venezia?	Dove posso prendere la **navetta** per l'hotel Hilton Venezia?

Nah-veh-tah

Transportation Method	Mezzo di trasporto
Taxis are usually the best **method of transport** to go to the city center.	I taxi sono in genere il miglior **mezzo di trasporto** per raggiungere il centro città.

"Mezzo di trasporto" is one of those basic and general words you will want to add to your vocabulary. Anything from a cab to a rented car is a transportation method and is, therefore, a "mezzo di trasporto". Repeat with me: "Meh-dzoh dee trahs-porh-toh".

Bus	Autobus
Where can I take a **bus** downtown?	Dove posso prendere un **autobus** per andare in centro?

Please, remember the sound for the Italian "u" is like "oo" in English. Other than that, this should be an easy one.

How-toh-boos

As you have just landed in Venice, you should be aware of the different transportation methods available to go to the city center. In fact, you can choose between several options, either by land or by boat. As such, you could get a bus or a water bus (Vaporetto – vah-poh-reh-toh); a taxi or a water taxi (Taxi d'acqua).

If you are staying in Venice city center, you should also notice that, if you decide to get a taxi, bus or train these will only take you to the main train station or car park and you will need to continue your journey by boat (or on foot).

Let's go back to our lesson. If you are traveling with the family, you might want to rent a car.

Car rental	Noleggio auto
Where is the **car rental**?	Dov'è il **noleggio auto**?

Noh-leh-joh how-toh

Driving license	Patente di guida
I will need a **driver's license**.	Mi servirà la **patente di guida**.

Pah-tehn-teh dee gwih-dah

www.LearnLikeNatives.com

You have finally made it to your hotel. The panorama is wonderful and your room has a nice view of the canal and a beautiful little square. Can you imagine it? Great! Me too! You will be able to get some rest soon, but first you have to check-in.

Check-in	Check-in
I would like to **check into** my room.	Desidero effettuare il **check-in** per la mia camera.

As you can see, check-in is used in Italian as well, and it's pronounced in the same way.

Reservation	Prenotazione
Under whose name is the reservation?	A che nome è la **prenotazione?**

Preh-noh-tah-tzeeoh-neh

Key	Chiave
Here is your **key**.	Ecco la **chiave**.

Kee-ah-veh

Depending on which hotel you stay at, it might be a standard key (chiave), a keycard (carta elettronica), or a pin code (codice pin). In any case, you can use the general word "chiave", and everyone will be able to understand.

Elevator	Ascensore
The **Elevator** is down the hall.	L'**ascensore** è in fondo al corridoio.

Ah-shen-soh-reh

Floor	Piano
Our room is on the 7th **floor.**	La nostra camera è al settimo **piano**.

I am sure you already know how to pronounce this word: Pee-ah-noh. Please be aware that the same word means "slowly" and "floor".

Hey! I know you can't wait to see your room, so come on, open the door!

Look around your room. I am sure there is a nice comfy bed, maybe a flat-screen, and a closet. You stop a minute to admire the sunset from your window. But now it's time to learn the name of the things around you.

Bed	Letto
Honey! Our **bed** is huge!	Tesoro! Il nostro **letto** è enorme.

Leh-toh

TV	TV / Televisione
Is it a smart **TV**?	È una smart **TV**?

Teh-leh-vee-siho-neh

Closet	Armadio
I'll put the suitcases inside the **closet**.	Metterò le valigie dentro all'**armadio**.

Ahr-mah-deeoh

At this point, you should be able to properly pronounce the "r".

Now let's go to see the bathroom. Hot tubs are not so common in Italy, but you will definitely find a shower and a toilet. Just in case you have to report any problems with the pipes, you may want to learn a few words and sentences to deal with possible water leaks.

www.LearnLikeNatives.com

Shower	Doccia
We have a massage **shower**.	Abbiamo una **doccia** idromassaggio.

Doh-chah

Toilet	Water
Two bathrooms! We have a **toilet** each.	Due bagni! Abbiamo un **water** ciascuno.

Vah-tehr.

Yeah, that's right. I know you use "water" to mean drinkable water, but in Italian, it is a little bit different. A "water" is the toilet! And, of course, also the pronunciation is different "Vah-tehr".

Sink	Lavandino
I will put my things by the **sink**.	Metterò le mie cose vicino al **lavandino**.

Lah-vahn-dee-noh

Towels	Asciugamani

www.LearnLikeNatives.com

Hello! I need more **towels**.	Salve! Ho bisogno di più **asciugamani**.

Ah-shoo-gah-mah-nee

Pillows	Cuscini
I also need 2 more **pillows**.	Mi servono anche altri 2 **cuscini**.

Practice these last two with me:

Ah-shooh-gah-mah-nee

Kooh-sheeh-noh

It turns out that my girlfriend always uses four pillows, and I always need some extra towels. As such, we do need those two sentences to survive when traveling.

Mini fridge	Frigobar
Is there a **mini-fridge** in my room?	C'è il **frigobar** nella mia stanza?

Free-goh bar

You have been lucky. You have got such a nice room! So, are you ready to look at a short conversation?

Concierge: *Hello! How can I help you?*

Salve! Come posso aiutarla?

Dan: *Hello! I think my sink is leaking.*

Salve! Credo di avere un lavandino che perde.

Concierge: *I will send someone right away!*

Mando subito qualcuno!

Dan: *Thanks. I appreciate your help.*

Grazie. Apprezzo il vostro aiuto.

Concierge: *I am sorry for the inconvenience. Is there anything I can do to make your stay more pleasant?*

Mi scuso per l'inconveniente. Posso fare altro per rendere il vostro soggiorno più confortevole?

Dan: *Now that you mention it, I notice my room does not have a mini-fridge.*

                Ora che ci penso, ho notato che la mia camera non ha il frigobar.

Concierge: *Of course! Anything else?*

                Certo! Serve altro?

Dan: *I'd like a couple more towels, and one extra pillow, please.*

                Vorrei qualche asciugamano in più e un altro cuscino, per favore.

Concierge: *Sure! Just in case you need more pillows, you have an extra inside the closet.*

                Certamente! Se ha bisogno di altri cuscini, ce n'è uno in più nell'armadio.

Dan: *Good to know! Thanks!*

                Buono a sapersi! Grazie!

Concierge: *Is there anything else I can do for you today?*

                Posso fare altro per aiutarla?

Dan: *I am okay. Thank you very much.*

No non c'è altro. Grazie mille.

Concierge: *I will send help right away. Again, sorry for the inconvenience.*

Manderò qualcuno immediatamente. Mi scuso nuovamente per il disagio causato.

Dan: *It is all good. Thanks for your help.*

Non c'è problema. Grazie dell'aiuto.

Concierge: *Thank you for being our guest!*

Grazie di aver scelto il nostro hotel.

Perfect! I think we are all set for a nice stay! Ready to go out and explore the city?

Chapter 4 – I Am Happy When the Sun is Shining

You are finally here, where you have always dreamed to be. The weather is wonderful, and the sounds of church bells ringing and of the boat passing by the narrow canals are amplified in your room. A small orchestra is playing in the distance. This is all you ever wanted, and now you are ready to go out and discover everything that this amazing place has to offer.

Before heading out, let's check the weather.

Weather	Clima
How's the **weather** in Venice?	Com'è il **clima** a Venezia?

Clee-mah

We are going to start learning the name of seasons.

Spring	Primavera
Flowers are blooming. **Spring** is here.	I fiori stanno sbocciando. È arrivata la **primavera.**

Pree-mah-veh-rah

Summer	Estate
In the tropics, it always feels like **summer**.	Ai tropici, è sempre **estate**.

Ehs-tah-teh

Again, remember to work on your "open" vowels. The clearer the sound, the better.

Fall	Autunno
Look at the trees and their **fall** colors.	Guarda gli alberi e i colori dell'**autunno**.

How-tooh-noh

As you know, the weather can change quickly. Generally, summer is hot and dry, while winter is cold, but sometimes the weather can change many times a day.

Cloud	Nuvola
Look at that big **cloud**.	Guarda quella grande **nuvola.**

Nooh-voh-lah

Sun	Sole
The **sun** was too strong.	Il **sole** picchiava troppo forte.

Soh-leh

Rain	Pioggia
The **rain** came without a warning.	La **pioggia** è arrivata all'improvviso.

Pyoh-jah

Storm	Temporale
Before we knew, the **storm** was here.	Prima che ce ne rendessimo conto, è arrivato il **temporale**.

Tehm-pohr-ah-leh

Is there any popular movie you can think of? I can remember quite a few.

Wind	Vento

The **wind** was so strong that the windows were moving.	Il **vento** era così forte che sbatteva le finestre.

Vehn-toh

Degrees	Gradi

We were under 0 **degrees**.	Stavamo a meno di 0 **gradi**.

Grah-dee

Something to keep in mind is that the metric system is very common outside the US. So depending on your destination, download a unit converter could be very useful.

Hurricane	Uragano

The **hurricane** wrecked it all.	L'**uragano** ha distrutto tutto.

Ooh-rah-gah-noh. It's the perfect word to practice your single "r" soft sound with.

Sunglasses	Occhiali da sole

I left my **sunglasses** on the bed!	Ho lasciato i miei **occhiali da sole** sopra il letto!

www.LearnLikeNatives.com

Ohk-ee-ah-lee dah soh-leh

Hat	Cappello
That's a nice **hat**!	Che bel **cappello**!

Kah-peh-loh

Sunscreen	Crema solare
Did you bring **sunscreen**?	Hai portato la **crema solare**?

Kreh-mah soh-lah-reh

Umbrella	Ombrello
Let's take the **umbrella**.	Prendiamo l'**ombrello**.

Ohm-breh-loh

Raincoat	Impermeabile
It is necessary to bring your **raincoat**.	Devi portare il tuo **impermeabile**.

Ihm-pehr-meh-ah-bee-leh

This is a very useful word. It is used to indicate a raincoat or just to indicate that something is waterproof: "Impermeabile". Keep it in mind! You may want to get one next time you go shopping.

Talking about it, why don't we go on a shopping spree?

Seller: *Hello! Good afternoon. How can I help you?*

Salve! Buon pomeriggio. Come posso aiutarla?

Ken: *Hey! Good afternoon. I would like to buy some things.*

Salve! Buon pomeriggio. Desidero comprare alcune cose.

Seller: *Sure! What do you have in mind?*

Certo! Ha in mente qualcosa in particolare?

Ken: *Everything. I need an umbrella, sunglasses, a raincoat... everything.*

Tutto. Ho bisogno di un ombrello, occhiali da sole, impermeabile... di tutto.

Seller: *Oh, I see. Did the hurricane catch you off guard?*

Oh, capisco. L'uragano l'ha colta di sorpresa?

Ken: *Yes. Totally. It has been crazy. Sun goes, and rain comes. Repeatedly.*

Sì. Completamente. È pazzesco. Il sole sparisce e inizia a diluviare. Continuamente.

Seller: *I am sorry to hear that. I will help you, gladly.*

Ne sono spiacente. Sarò felice di aiutarla.

Ken: *Thanks! What raincoats do you have?*

Grazie! Che impermeabili avete?

Seller: *I have these raincoats. Good quality and they protect you down to 0 degrees.*

Abbiamo questi impermeabili. Sono di buona qualità e proteggono fino a 0 gradi.

Ken: *Awesome! What about umbrellas?*

Perfetto! E ombrelli?

Seller: *I have many. It depends on what size you are looking for.*

Ne abbiamo molti. Dipende dalla grandezza che preferisce.

Ken:	*Just a couple of small umbrellas. Something easy to carry.*
	Solo un paio di ombrelli piccoli. Qualcosa facile da trasportare.
Seller:	*Sure! Why don't you come with me to pick sunglasses?*
	Va bene! Perchè non viene con me a scegliere degli occhiali da sole?
Ken:	*Glad to! I will follow you.*
	Ne sarei felice! La seguo.
Seller:	*Very well. This way, please.*
	Molto bene. Da questa parte per favore.

I hope you remembered to bring sunscreen. It has finally stopped raining, so we are going out for some sightseen and I do not want you to get a nasty sunburn. Remember to bring everything with you. As always, the most important thing is to be prepared.

Chapter 5 – I Have So Many Stories to Tell

Do you know what I love most about life? That everyone has a story to tell! And many of these stories are about traveling. It is all about exploring new cultures, meeting new people, and stepping out of your comfort zone.

I remember when I was in the cradle of the Renaissance: the beautiful Florence. Everything seemed perfect. The location was terrific: close to tourist attractions. Even our hotel's architecture was amazing, and the panorama was breathtaking. So, everything was perfect… until I opened my room's door and discovered that my toilet was inside the shower.

Trust me, I am not picky. As the location was perfect and everything was already paid for, I decided to spend the night there. Well, I must admit that my optimism vanished after I went to the bathroom in the middle of the night and got my socks soaking wet from the shower. Needless to say, this is still a GREAT and funny story to tell my friends and one of those things I will remember forever.

If you are a storyteller, as I am, you will need few more lessons to broaden your vocabulary and delight your friends–even your new local friends–with the crazy stories of your little adventures. To help you bring your stories to life, you will use two different verbal tenses. It is something you probably already know, as you should have studied in school. Don't worry. We won't focus on grammar, okay? Instead, we will see some practical examples.

Italian uses two past tenses to describe actions that happened in the past:

- Imperfetto
- Passato Prossimo

Let's start with the first one: past simple, which in Italian is called "imperfetto". It is close to "undefined past". It's used to talk about events that took place in the past, as well as actions that occurred multiple times.

First of all, in Italian, verb conjugation is done by changing the ending of the verb. Verbs are divided into 3 different categories, called "coniugazioni" - conjugations. Each one is characterized by a specific ending in its infinitive form:

- First conjugation: Verbs ending in -ARE (like viaggiare)
- Second conjugation: Verbs ending in -ERE (like credere)
- Third conjugation: Verbs ending in -IRE (like partire)

This applies to all regular verbs, and it is very important because, as you will see using the below table, you will be able to conjugate every other verb part of the same conjugation.

Please also note that, as you do in English, in Italian you can merge all the 3rd person singular pronouns. For your convenience, this is what we will do here.

We will start with a very useful verb: "viaggiare" – to travel.

To travel	Viaggiare	Root	Termination
I travelled	Io viaggiavo	Viaggi-	Are changes to "avo"
You travelled	Tu viaggiavi		Are changes to "avi"
He/She/It travelled	Lui/Lei/Egli viaggiava		Are changes to "ava"
We travelled	Noi viaggiavamo		Are changes to "avamo"
You travelled	Voi viaggiavate		Are changes to "avate"
They travelled	Loro viaggiavano		Are changes to "avano"

The root of all regular verbs never changes. As you can see, the root is the part preceding the infinitive ending. So, for example, in "Viaggiare" the root is "Viaggi-". As we said, the root always remains the same, and different endings are added to denote the person, number or tense.

The same thing will happen for the group of verbs ending in "ere", as in "conoscere" (root "conosc-") or "credere" (root "cred-"), and for the "ire" conjugation, as in "dormire" (root "dorm-") or "finire" (root "fin-").

Come on! It may look hard to start with, but it's not that complicated. You just need to remember the rules and practice a little bit more.

Let's see few examples.

As a boy, I traveled all the time.	Da ragazzo, viaggiavo per il mondo.
Last year, my dad traveled a lot for work.	L'anno scorso, mio padre viaggiava spesso per lavoro.
We traveled every two months.	Noi viaggiavamo ogni due mesi.
They traveled a lot before having kids.	Loro viaggiavano molto prima di avere figli.

Have you noticed it? In every sentence, all the actions have already happened: when I was young, last year, in the past. Past simple is for things that happened in the past.

Notice how the verb in these sentences, could also be read as "used to travel" instead of "traveled". You could consider it a clue–every time you can change the English verb in the past tense to "used to + verb", you are in the presence of Italian past "imperfetto".

As a boy, I used to travel all the time.	Da ragazzo, viaggiavo sempre.
Last year, my dad used to travel a lot for work.	L'anno scorso, mio padre viaggiava spesso per lavoro.
We used to travel every two months.	Noi viaggiavamo ogni due mesi.
They used to travel a lot before having kids.	Loro viaggiavano molto prima di avere figli.

Let's see what the differences are with the second conjugation "ere".

To believe	Credere	Root	Termination

I believed	Io credevo		Ere changes to "evo"
You believed	Tu credevi		Ere changes to "evi"
He/She/It believed	Lui/Lei/Egli credeva	Cred-	Ere changes to "eva"
We believed	Noi credevamo		Ere changes to "evamo"
You believed	Voi credevate		Ere changes to "evate"
They believed	Loro credevano		Ere changes to "evano"

Let's practice with some examples.

When I was little, I believed in fairy tales.	Da piccola, credevo alle favole.
She believed whatever she was told.	Lei credeva a tutto quello che le dicevano.
You believed in impossible things.	Voi credevate a cose impossibili.

| They believed I was a policeman. | Loro credevano fossi un poliziotto. |

I am sure you will use this verb quite a bit. After all, this is how many funny stories begin–I believed…

Now up to the next one: to discover.

To discover	**Scoprire**	Root	**Termination**
I discovered	Io scoprivo	Scopr-	Ire changes to "ivo"
You discovered	Tu scoprivi		Ire changes to "ivi"
He/She/It discovered	Lui/Lei/Egli scoprivano		Ire changes to "iva"
We discovered	Noi scoprivamo		Ire changes to "ivamo"
You discovered	Voi scoprivate		Ire changes to "ivate"
They discovered	Loro scoprivano		Ire changes to "ivano"

Can you understand this better now? Let's see some sentences.

As a child, I discovered new things every day.	Da bambino, scoprivo cose nuove ogni giorno.
In 1770 Captain Cook discovered Australia.	Nel 1770 il capitano Cook scopriva l'Australia.
You discovered new ways to surprise me, day after day.	Tu scoprivi nuovi modi di sorprendermi, giorno dopo giorno.
They gradually discovered the truth.	A poco a poco loro scoprivano la verità.

As we explained earlier, for all regular verbs ending in "ire", you only need to find the root and then add the correct termination.

How are you doing so far? Don't worry. We will keep working on this a little longer, using more examples.

Our next verb is "to have". "To have" and "to be" are fundamental in building complex sentences, but they are irregular verbs both in English and in Italian, so the rules described above are not applicable to these verbs. Let's take a look.

To have	**Avere**
I had	Io avevo

You had	Tu avevi
He/She/It had	Lui/Lei/Egli aveva
We had	Noi avevamo
You had	Voi avevate
They had	Loro avevano

Are you ready to look at some examples?

I had high expectations when I was young.	Avevo grandi aspettative quando ero piccolo.
You had everything you asked for.	Tu avevi tutto ciò che chiedevi.
She had a beautiful dress.	Lei aveva un bel vestito.
We had so much to be grateful.	Avevamo tanto di cui essere grati.

The next verb is a little more complex: "to be". In English, as well as in Italian, is the main verb that indicates existence. It is an auxiliary verb and its purpose is to help other verbs conjugate in compound tenses. In other words, it helps to create more complex sentences and tenses.

There is also another verb that can sometimes be used with the same meaning of "to be": "stare" – "to stay". While in

English "to stay" is only used to describe your location, in Italian it can also be used to describe a state of being.

To be	Essere	To stay	Stare
I was	Io ero	I stayed	Io stavo
You were	Tu eri	You stayed	Tu stavi
He/She/It was	Lui/Lei/Egli era	He/She/It stayed	Lui/Lei/Egli stava
We were	Noi eravamo	We stayed	Noi stavamo
You were	Voi eravate	You stayed	Voi stavate
They were	Loro erano	They stayed	Loro stavano

You may be wondering: when should I use what? So here are some examples to explain the use of the verb "essere" (to be):

- To describe or identify someone or something. For example: "Quello era Giovanni." – "That was Giovanni."; "Voi eravate soldati." – "You were soldiers."
- To describe something or someone. As in, "Tu eri così bella." – "You were so beautiful." Or, "Loro erano davvero veloci." – "They were really quick."

- To speak about time, date, weather and similar. "Era in autunno." – "It was in the autumn."; "Erano circa le quattro del pomeriggio." – "It was around four in the afternoon."
- To decide or describe a location. "La festa era a casa di Natalia." – "The party was at Natalia's house"; "L'incontro era a San Francisco." – "The Summit was in San Francisco."

On the other side, the verb "stare" is used for these cases:

- To speak about locations. "Io stavo in California." – "I was in California."; "Loro stavano a casa tutto il tempo." – "They were at home all the time."
- To talk of someone's or something's state. "Lei stava sempre da sola." – "She was always alone."; "Loro stavano bene." – "They were fine."

Let's see some examples of the verb "essere".

I was so happy that night.	Ero così felice quella notte.
She was Prom Queen.	Lei era la Regina del Ballo.
We were young once.	Un tempo noi eravamo giovani.
They were invincible.	Loro erano invincibili.

Is it everything clear?

Let's move on to "stare".

I was going out when I realized I had no keys with me.	Io **stavo** per uscire quando ho realizzato di non avere la chiavi.
He was silent.	Lui **stava** in silenzio.
We were by the pool.	Noi **stavamo** vicino alla piscina.
I want to be with you.	Voglio **stare** con te.

As with any other language, Italian is all about structure and I promise it will get easier with some practice. As always, to help you get a better understanding, we will focus on sentences and conversations.

As we said at the beginning, there are two past tenses in Italian. We have already seen the past simple or "imperfetto", now let's move on to the recent past or "passato prossimo".

To create this tense, we need to learn how to create the past participle "participio passato".

As a general rule for the regular verbs, to create participio passato you will use the root of the verb with the ending:

- -ATO for the first conjugation -Are i.e. to learn "imparare" becomes "imparato": root impar-, -ato ending;
- -UTO for the second conjugation -Ere i.e. to learn "sapere" becomes "saputo": root sap-, -uto ending;
- -ITO for the third conjugation -Ire i.e. to learn "partire" becomes "partito": root part-, -ito ending.

Perhaps I could make that a little easier for you, with a table of few verbs conjugated at the past participle or "participio passato".

Verb	Participio Passato
To go – Andare	Andato
To learn – Imparare	Imparato
To eat – Mangiare	Mangiato
To travel – Viaggiare	Viaggiato
To think – Pensare	Pensato

To know – Sapere	Saputo
To have – Avere	Avuto
To believe – Credere	Creduto
To know – Sapere	Saputo
To want – Volere	Voluto
To keep – Tenere	Tenuto
To finish – Finire	Finito
To leave – Partire	Partito
To exit – Uscire	Uscito
To understand – Capire	Capito
To feel – Sentire	Sentito

Now let's move on to the recent past or "passato prossimo". Now that you know hot to the participio passato works, you'll see how easy it will be with Passato Prossimo.

The similarity is in the way you form a compound tense. This tense is used to describe actions that happened at a particular time in the past. In addition, you should be aware that to form the past, you will need to use one of the auxiliary verbs: to have (avere) or to be (essere) at the present + Past Participle

It will become clearer when we will see some practical applications.

To travel	Viaggiare	Root	Termination
I traveled	Io ho viaggiato	Viaggi-	Present tense I have + Are changes to "ato"
You traveled	Tu hai viaggiato		Present tense You have + Are changes to "ato"
He/She/It traveled	Lui/Lei/Egli ha viaggiato		Present tense He/She/It has + Are changes to "ato"

We traveled	Noi abbiamo viaggiato		Present tense We have + Are changes to "ato"
You traveled	Voi avete viaggiato		Present tense You have + Are changes to "ato"
They traveled	Loro hanno viaggiato		Present tense They have + Are changes to "ato"

As you can see, to form the past, we used the auxiliary verb "avere". At the past "viaggiare" became "viaggiato", but you will need to add the verb "avere" (conjugated at the present tense) in front.

I traveled to Spain last year.	Io ho viaggiato in Spagna lo scorso anno.
She traveled through the entire continent.	Lei ha viaggiato attraverso tutto il continente.
You traveled a lot during the last two months.	Tu hai viaggiato un sacco negli ultimi due mesi.
We traveled to Mexico during the summer.	Noi abbiamo viaggiato in Messico durante l'estate.

Are you getting any better at this? Let's keep working on it.

To believe	Credere	Root	Termination
I believed	Io ho creduto	Cred-	Present tense I have + Are changes to "uto"
You believed	Tu hai creduto		Present tense You have + Are changes to "uto"
He/She/It believed	Lui/Lei/Egli ha creduto		Present tense He/She/It has + Are changes to "uto"
We believed	Noi abbiamo creduto		Present tense We have + Are changes to "uto"
You believed	Voi avete creduto		Present tense You have + Are changes to "uto"
They believed	Loro hanno creduto		Present tense They have + Are changes to "uto"

www.LearnLikeNatives.com

As always, don't worry. Practice makes perfect! I am sure you will be able to use correctly these tenses very soon. Just keep practicing, ok?

I believed every word he said.	Ho creduto ad ogni parola che lui diceva.
She believed that I did it on purpose.	Lei ha creduto lo avessi fatto apposta.
We believed in progress.	Abbiamo creduto nel progresso.
They believed in me.	Loro hanno creduto in me.

Can you believe how easy it is? Does that make sense? Let's see one more verb.

To finish	**Finire**	**Root**	**Termination**
I finished	Io ho finito	Fin-	Present tense I have + Are changes to "ito"
You finished	Tu hai finito		Present tense You have + Are changes to "ito"
He/She/It finished	Lui/Lei/Egli ha finito		Present tense He/She/It has +

			Are changes to "ito"
We finished	Noi abbiamo finito		Present tense We have + Are changes to "ito"
You finished	Voi avete finito		Present tense You have + Are changes to "ito"
They finished	Loro hanno finito		Present tense They have + Are changes to "ito"

Can you see how the terminations shift? Let's see some examples.

I finished writing my presentation.	Io ho finito di scrivere la mia presentazione.
He finished the marathon.	Lui ha finito la maratona.
You finished your PHD.	Voi avete finito il dottorato.

They finished the work earlier.	Loro hanno finito prima il lavoro.

Did you see how quickly you are improving your knowledge? It becomes easy to understand. Now let's have a look at the irregular verb "to have" or "avere".

To have	**Avere**
I had	Io ho avuto
You had	Tu hai avuto
He/She/It had	Lui/Lei/Egli ha avuto
We had	Noi abbiamo avuto
You had	Voi avete avuto
They had	Loro hanno avuto

Let's see some applications.

I had such a great night. It was magical.	Io ho avuto una serata meravigliosa. È stato magico.
You had everything you asked for.	Tu hai avuto tutto quello che desideravi.

She had a beautiful dress.	Lei ha avuto un vestito bellissimo.
We had so much to be grateful.	Noi abbiamo avuto così tanto di cui essere grati.

We are now going to conjugate the verbs "to be" and "to stay". Keep in mind that, as we saw in the verb conjugations above, both "to be" and "to have" are used as auxiliary verbs to create more complex sentences. As a consequence, it is very important to learn to correctly conjugate these verbs at the past "passato prossimo".

To be	**Essere**	**Stare**
I was	Io sono stato	Io sono stato
You were	Tu sei stato	Tu sei stato
He/She/It was	Lui/Lei/Egli è stato	Lui/Lei/Egli è stato
We were	Noi siamo stati	Noi siamo stati
You were	Voi siete stati	Voi siete stati
They were	Loro sono stati	Loro sono stati

As you can see, there is no difference in the "passato prossimo" of "to be" and "to stay". A closer look will show how you are in fact using both verbs: to be as auxiliary and to stay (-ato for singular and -ati for plural) as ending.

Let's practice a bit more.

I was a Prom Queen.	Io sono stata la Reginetta del Ballo.
He was a great athlete.	Lui è stato un grande atleta.
We were a great team.	Noi siamo stati una squadra fantastica.
They were young once.	Loro sono stati giovani.

Now that we have learned "to have" and "to be" in the past tense, we can start to build more complex sentences.

First, let me give you an example:

When it had finished raining, I kept walking.

As you can see, you combine "had" ("have" in the past tense) with the past participle of another regular verb to indicate two actions that are finished, one after the other.

In Italian, that structure remains the same.

Quando ha finito di piovere, ho continuato a camminare.

I understand you may be a little confused now. Do not rush. Let's see some more examples.

When he had awakened, she was already gone.	*Quando si è svegliato, lei se ne era già andata.*
Once they had found the ball, they came back to play.	*Quando hanno trovato il Pallone, hanno ricominciato a giocare.*
As soon as I had studied, I took five minutes for myself.	*Appena ho finite di studiare, ho preso cinque minuti per me stesso.*

Thanks to our conversation, you will have the chance to understand how all these elements fit together.

Kate: *Hello! I am so glad you came back. Did you have a good summer?*

Ciao! Sono così felice tu sia ritornato. Hai passato una bella estate?

Alex: *Hi! I am glad as well. It was a fun summer.*

Ciao! Anche io ne sono felice. È stata un'estate divertente.

Kate: *Great! Tell me everything!*

Fantastico! Raccontami tutto!

Alex: *I went to Italy.*

Sono andato in l'Italia.

Kate: *That's nice. Did you go by train or plane?*

Che bello. Sei andato in auto o in aereo?

Alex: *I flew there and then I rented a car.*

Sono andato in aereo e poi ho nolleggiato un'auto.

Kate: *Good idea! What were you doing during the day?*

Buona idea! Cosa facevi durante il giorno?

Alex: *When I was not driving, I visited all the main touristic sites.*

Quando non guidavo, ho visitato tutti i principali luoghi turistici.

Kate: *It sounds like you have been very busy!*

Sembra tu sia stato molto impegnato!

Alex:

Yeah, I was. And do you remember how much I love the rain?

Kate: Si, hai ragione. E ti ricordi quanto amo la pioggia?

Sure.

Certo.

Alex: *It turns out one night it was raining in Florence, but I had bought tickets to see a movie.*

Una notte Pioveva a Firenze, ma avevo comprato due biglietti per andare a vedere un film.

Kate: *Such a pity!*

Che peccato!

Alex: *I have always had that thing with rain.*

Mi è sempre piaciuta la pioggia.

Kate: *Indeed.*

Lo so.

Do you feel like an expert at putting phrases together? You should. We have come a long way. Besides, you are going to need those skills now because we are going on an adventure.

Chapter 6 – So Many Roads and So Many Places

Personally, I love walking. When I was younger - and single - I used to wear my headphones and walk around for miles and miles in every new city I visited. Since I got a girlfriend, I put the headphones away and enjoyed long chats while we visited places together. We usually take lots of photos, a lot of them are pictures of me taking pictures of her, or beautiful panoramas. I do enjoy taking pictures of my loved one under different shades and lights. Have you ever noticed how every city has its own colors and vibes?

All right, let's go back to business. Tell me: what do you usually like to visit first when exploring a new city? I am here to help you get anywhere you want to go. Why don't we start with the basics?

Museum	Museo
Where is the Vatican **Museum**?	Dove si trova il **Museo** del Vaticano?

Mooh-she-oh

The first syllable is easy. Just think at the sound a cow makes, "moooo-seh-oh".

Square	Piazza
How can I get to Venezia **Square**?	Come posso arrivare in **piazza** Venezia?

Pee-ah-tzah

Avenue	Viale
What can I find on Trastevere **avenue**?	Cosa posso trovare in **viale** Trastevere?

Vee-ah-leh

Monuments	Monumento
Rome is rich in history and **monuments.**	Roma è ricca di storia e **monumenti.**

Moh-nooh-mehn-toh

Park	Parco
Park Doria Pamphili is in Rome.	Il **parco** Doria Pamphili è a Roma.

Pahr-koh

Church	Chiesa

| They gave me this **church** as a reference. | Come punto di riferimento mi hanno dato questa **chiesa**. |

Kee-eh-zah

Not to be disrespectful, but traveling is not just about history and monuments. It is also about having fun and experiencing the true local culture, as well as going to bars and clubs.

Bar	Bar
Where is this **bar**?	Dove si trova questo **bar**?

Here it's another one! Globalization scores again!

Now that you have learned the name of some places, let's go there together.

Across	Dall'altro lato
You can find them **across** the avenue.	Lo puoi trovare **dall'altro lato** della strada.

Dahl ahl-troh lah-toh

In front of	Davanti a
He is waiting **in front of** the statue.	Lui sta aspettando **davanti alla** statua.

Dah-vahn-tee

Opposite	Opposto
We were walking in the **opposite** direction.	Stiamo camminando in senso **opposto.**

Oh-pohs-toh

Street	Strada
You can find it down the **street.**	Lo puoi trovare in fondo alla **strada.**

Strah-dah

Blocks	Quartiere/Isolato
How many **blocks** are left?	Quanti **isolati** ci mancano?

Kwuar-teeheh-reh / Ee-zoh-lah

Subway	Metropolitana
We can get there by **subway.**	Possiamo prendere la **metropolitana.**

This is a long word: Meh-troh-poh-lih-tah-nah

Mall	Centro commerciale

| What kind of **mall** would you like to visit? | Che genere di **centro commerciale** vorresti visitare? |

Chehn-troh Koh-mehr-cha-leh

Recommend	Consigli
What can you **recommend?**	Cosa **consigli?**

Kohn-see-glee

"Consigli" is a general word for "suggestions". So, whenever you are out of ideas, just remember this one. In Italian, this can also be translated as "suggerimenti" or "raccomandazioni".

In preparation for your next holiday, you have already learned so much! I am sure you will have no problems at all in getting around. You now know how to get a taxi, rent a car, ask for directions and recommendations. We are almost done with this chapter, we just have to practice a little bit more.

Front desk (Reception): *Hello! How can I help you?*

Salve! Come posso aiutarla?

Allen: I would like some recommendations for places to visit.

Vorrei qualche consiglio sui luoghi da visitare.

Front desk: Very well. What type of place did you have in mind? A club, a museum?

Va bene. A che genere di posti pensava? Un club, un museo...?

Allen: I have heard that you have beautiful squares and monuments in this city.

Ho sentito che avete piazza e monumenti meravigliosi in questa città.

Front desk: That is true. Sadly, most cultural attractions are across town.

È vero. Purtoppo però, la maggior parte delle attrazioni culturali sono dall'altro lato della città.

Philip: Oh, I see. Could you give me some directions, please?

	Oh, capisco. Potrebbe darmi qualche indicazione, per favore?
Front desk:	*Sure! Would you like to travel by car or take the subway?*
	Certamente! Desidera viaggiare in auto o prendere la metropolitana?
Philip:	*I would rather take a subway and walk.*
	Preferisco prendere la metropolitana e camminare.
Front desk:	*Very well. The subway is only 3 blocks away.*
	Molto bene. La stazione della metropolitana dista solo 3 isolati.
Philip:	*Perfect! How do I get there?*
	Perfetto! Come posso arrivarci?
Front desk:	*You only have to go down this street, take a right, and walk straight for 3 blocks.*

	Deve solo proseguire lungo questa strada, svoltare a destra, e camminare dritto per 3 isolati.
Philip:	*That sounds easy. Thank you very much!*
	Sembra facile. Grazie mille!
Front desk:	*All right, then. After you get to the subway, go to the mainline and take a train to Termini station.*
	Perfetto, allora. Quando arriva alla metropolitana, vada alla linea principale e prenda il treno per la stazione Termini.
Philip:	*Very good. I appreciate your help.*
	Va bene. La ringrazio del suo aiuto.
Front desk:	*My pleasure. Have a nice day.*
	Il piacere è mio. Buona giornata.
Allen:	*Likewise. Bye.*
	Anche a lei. Arrivederci.

Ready to walk around the city and get lost in its little streets? I'm sure you can't wait. Then you'd better get ready. Go out and have fun. Who knows how many funny stories you will be able to tell once back from your trip!

Although now I am getting a bit hungry. Sorry, what did you say? Should we go and grab a bite to eat?

Chapter 7 – Eat, Travel, Love

Food is one of my favorite things and so, in my opinion, it is the best part of traveling. Taste good wine or eat typical regional dishes is an awesome way to learn a bit more about the culture and history of each place you visit. The sense of taste and smell guide us on an imaginary journey that can lead you out of the touristic itinerary. You can enjoy the view on the hills while drinking Prosecco in the Veneto region, eat a delicious pizza in Naples's older pizzeria; try Arancini (stuffed rice balls) in beautiful Sicily or experience the real gelato. Everywhere you go, flavors are unique and that is what makes them an important part of traveling.

It is precisely for this reason that I want you to have the best time ever. I am sure you will have plenty of opportunities to order some food, for dinner at the restaurant or at the bar for breakfast. So, that is where we will start from. You are probably already aware that most traditional places won't have a translated menu. Let's start this chapter.

Restaurant	Ristorante
Let's go into that **restaurant.**	Andiamo in quel **ristorante.**

Rees-toh-rahn-teh

www.LearnLikeNatives.com

It is very similar to the English word, just remember to put emphasis on the open vowels.

Table	Tavolo
Table for 4, please.	**Tavolo** per 4, per favore.

Tah-voh-loh

Dish of the day	Piatto del giorno
Do you want to hear **today's special**?	Vuole sapere qual è il **piatto del giorno**?

Pee-ah-toh dehl jorh-noh

Many restaurants will offer a "piatto del giorno" or "specialità", often scribed on an erasable board placed just outside. It varies from day to day, usually depending on available ingredients. These usually "off the menu" or chef recommendations are frequently a good choice to try something different.

If you struggle to make up your mind, or just would like a recommendation, you could ask your waiter for a suggestion.

Suggestion	Raccomandazione
What are your **suggestions**?	Qual è la sua **raccomandazione**?

www.LearnLikeNatives.com

Rah-coh-mahn-dah-tzioh-neh

Portion	Porzione
I want a **portion** of fries.	Vorrei una **porzione** di patate fritte.

Pohr-tzeeoh-neh

This is becoming easier with time, huh?

Fork	Forchetta
I dropped my **fork.**	Mi è caduta la **forchetta.**

Fohr-keh-tah

Spoon	Cucchiaio
Can I get a **spoon**?	Posso avere un **cucchiaio**?

Coohk-eeah-eeoh

Do you remember this sound? I am sure you will find this very easy as the Italian "ch" is pronounced as a hard "K" in English, like in "cook".

Knife	Coltello
I will need a meat **knife.**	Mi servirà un **coltello** per la carne.

Cohl-the-loh

Plate	Piatto
Can you bring an extra **plate**?	Potrebbe portarmi un altro **piatto**?

Pee-ah-toh

Starter	Antipasto
Do you want a **starter**?	Vuoi un **antipasto**?

Ant-ee-pahs-toh

First course	Primo (piatto)
I will have pasta carbonara as **first course**...	Prendo pasta alla carbonara di **primo**...

Pree-moh pee-ah-toh

Second course	Secondo (piatto)
...and steak with chips as second course	...e bistecca con le patate fritte di **secondo**...

Seh-kohn-doh pee-ah-toh

Dessert	Dolce

| Of course, I want a **dessert.** | Certo, vorrei il **dolce.** |

Dohl-ceh

Italian menus are usually divided into several categories which indicate different courses:

- Antipasto (starter), such as meat and cheese platters or bruschetta
- Primo (first course), which consist of pasta or rice
- Secondo (second course), is meat or fish with a side (contorno – kohn-tohr-noh) of vegetables
- Dolce or dessert.

You will also see that many people go for a drink and a bite before dinner time. This is called "aperitivo" – ah-peh-ree-tee-voh and usually consists of a glass of wine or soft drink with a small amount of food (i.e. olives, crisps, nuts, etc). Nowadays, in big towns like Milan or Bologna, aperitivo can easily become dinner as many places offer a rich complimentary buffet included in the price of the drink.

| Well-cooked | Ben cotto/a |
| I want my steak **well-cooked.** | Voglio che la mia bistecca sia **ben cotta.** |

Behn Coh-tah

Behn - Bene means "good" or "well".

Medium	Media
I like my steak medium.	Mi piace la bistecca a cottura **media**.

Meh-dee-ah

If you like your steak medium rare, you should ask for "una bistecca al sangue". Sahn-gweh – sangue, literally means blood.

Vegan	Vegano
Do you have a vegan menu?	Avete un menu **vegano**?

Veh-gah-noh

Check	Conto
I want my **check**, please.	Mi porti il **conto**, per favore.

Kohn-toh

Are you getting hungry? Let's see a short conversation…

Waiter (Cameriere): *Good evening! Welcome to our restaurant. My name is Marco. How many are you?*

	Buona sera! Benvenuti nel nostro ristorante. Il mio nome è Marco. Quanti siete?
Mike:	*Hello! We have a reservation under Paulson. Table for 4.*
	Salve! Abbiamo una prenotazione a nome Paulson. Tavolo per 4.
Waiter:	*Yes, here you are. Come with me, please.*
	Si, eccola qui. Seguitemi, per favore.
Mike:	*I would like to order right away. We are starving.*
	Vorrei ordinare subito. Siamo affamati.
Waiter:	*Perfect. What would you like to order?*
	Perfetto. Cosa volete ordinare?
Mike:	*What are your suggestions?*
	Quali sono le sue raccomandazioni?
Waiter:	*The bruschetta as an appetizer. For the first course, we have saffron rice cooked with mixed vegetables.*

| | La bruschetta come antipaso. Come primo, abbiamo riso allo zafferano e verdure. |

Mike: *Sounds great! I want one of each. Also, a salad and two beef dishes.*

Sembra perfetto! Ne ordino uno di entrambi. Inoltre, un'insalata e due piatti di carne.

Waiter: *Do you want extra plates to share?*

Volete qualche piatto in più per condividere?

Mike: Yes, please.

Si, per favore.

Waiter: *Perfect. I will be back in a second with your plates, forks, and meat knives.*

Perfetto. Tornerò tra un attimo con i piatti, forchette e coltelli per la carne.

Mike: *Thank you very much.*

Grazie mille.

Waiter: *I'll be right back.*

Torno subito.

I think this is a very important chapter, and I am sure you found it easy. Did you manage to easily follow the above conversation?

So, what next? I really don't want to worry you, but you are about to feel a bit under the weather.

Chapter 8 – Being Sick Abroad!

Whenever I go abroad, I purchase a travel insurance. However, I always hope I won't need to make any claim. Being sick abroad can be scary. Nobody likes to be ill or wants that to ruin their vacation! However, it is always good to be prepared. Good communication skills can be the key to solve problems like this. So, let's get started.

Ill	Ammalato
I think I am **ill.**	Penso di essere **ammalato.**

Ah-mah-lah-toh

We previously saw "feeling ill" – "stare male". You can use both sentences: "stare male" or be (essere) "ammalato".

Cold	Raffreddore
I think I caught a **cold.**	Penso di aver preso il **raffreddore.**

Rah-freh-doh-reh

Cough	Tosse
I have a slight **cough.**	Ho un pò di **tosse.**

Toh-seh

Pain	Dolore
I took something for the **pain.**	Ho preso qualcosa per il **dolore.**

Doh-loh-reh

Practice those wide-open "o" sounds.

Migraine	Mal di testa
I have a **migraine.**	Ho **mal di testa.**

Mahl dee tehs-tah

Swollen	Gonfio/a
My throat is a bit **swollen.**	Ho la gola un poco **gonfia.**

Gohn-fee-oh/ah

Call the doctor	Chiama il dottore
Do you want to call the **doctor**?	Vuoi chiamare il **dottore**?

Doh-toh-reh

The word "dottore" is frequently used to ask help in case of an emergency. Please, practice this one and keep it in mind.

Doh-toh-reh

Emergency	Emergenza
I have an **emergency.**	C'è un'**emergenza.**

Eh-merh-jehn-tzah

Feel	Sentire (verb)
I **feel** a bit better.	Mi **sento** un poco meglio.

Sehn-toh

Patient	Paziente
I am a **patient** of Dr. Castello.	Sono un **paziente** del Dr. Castello.

Pah-tzee-ehn-teh

Blood pressure	Pressione sanguigna
The **blood pressure** is fine.	La **pressione sanguigna** va bene.

Preh-see-oh- neh sahn-gweeh-nyah

Pharmacy	Farmacia

www.LearnLikeNatives.com

| Where is the nearest **pharmacy**? | Dove si trova la **farmacia** più vicina? |

This is similar to English: "fahr-mah-cee-ah".

| Prescription | Prescrizione |
| I will need a **prescription.** | Avrò bisogno di una **prescrizione.** |

Prehs-kree-tzeeoh-neh

| Pills | Pillole |
| How many **pills** do I need? | Quante **pillole** devo prendere? |

Pee-loh-leh

We have already seen a similar scenario in a previous chapter, do you remember? So, this should be easy, as we have already covered it before. Are you ready to practice?

Liam: *Hello! I would like to speak to Dr. Castello.*

Salve! Vorrei parlare con il Dr. Castello.

Secretary (Segretaria): *Good afternoon, sir. What is your name?*

	Buon pomeriggio, signore. Come si chiama?
Liam:	*I am Liam Smith. One of your patients.*
	Sono Liam Smith. Uno dei suoi pazienti.
Secretary:	*Why do you call today?*
	Qual è il motivo della sua chiamata?
Liam:	*I have an emergency. My youngest son has a strong headache.*
	C'è un'emergenza. Il più piccolo dei miei figli ha un forte mal di testa,
Secretary:	*Any other symptoms?*
	Altri sintomi?
Liam:	*38°C fever. Also, complaints of abdominal pain.*
	Febbre a 38°C. Inoltre lamenta un dolore addominale.
Secretary:	*Is he allergic to something?*
	È allergico a qualcosa?

Liam:	*Yes. To gluten.*	
	Si. Al glutine.	
Secretary:	*Is he taking any prescriptions?*	
	Sta prendendo qualche prescrizione?	
Liam:	*No, just a dietary supplement.*	
	No, solo un integratore alimentare.	
Secretary:	*Come here at once and bring those pills.*	
	Venga qui immediatamente e porti quelle pillole.	

Yeah, I know what you think of all this: no parent with a celiac child would give him random pills! I agree with you, but sometimes it can happen.

I sincerely hope this book will hopefully help you to better understand and speak Italian. I love to travel and the diversity in people and styles, and I hope you enjoy the same things. I know how much independence and confidence you can gain by being able to communicate in more than one language. So, stay with me! We need you focused! Did I forget to mention something? You are now looking for a job.

Chapter 9 – Learn the Ropes

The research for a new employment can be exciting and frustrating at the same time. I used to work remotely–which allowed me to travel more–but I still had to find my own clients. If you are relocating or just thinking to spend a season in another city, get a job locally could be a great opportunity to have a better insight into a different culture.

As always, I will try to keep it simple.

Employment	Occupazione
I am looking for **employment.**	Sto cercando un'**occupazione.**

Oh-coo-pah-tzeeoh-neh

While this is what employment correctly translates to, it is more common to say you are looking for a job or "lavoro" – lah-voh-roh.

Employer	Datore di lavoro
My **employer** is very busy.	Il mio **datore di lavoro** è molto impegnato.

Dah-toh-reh dee lah-voh-roh

www.LearnLikeNatives.com

The most direct translation for "employer" is "datore di lavoro", but most people will just call it "boss" – capo. Cah-poh.

Employee	Dipendente
I am an **employee** of this shop.	Sono un **dipendente** di questo negozio.

Dee-pehn-dehn-teh

Permanent position	Posto fisso
I would like a **permanent position.**	Vorrei un **posto fisso.**

Pohs-toh Fee-soh

Temporary job	Lavoro temporaneo
I have a **temporary job.**	Ho un **lavoro temporaneo.**

Lah-voh-roh tehm-poh-rah-neoh

Salary	Stipendio
I want a **salary** increase.	Voglio un aumento dello **stipendio.**

Stee-pehn-dee-oh

Again, "salario" is the literal translation, but in fact, "stipendio" is normally used.

You will be asked your personal details many times, first name and second name. you have probably used this information already a dozen times. You will have to write these and other information on your CV, so let's review what we should already know. Just in case…

First name	Nome
What is your **first name**?	Qual è il tuo **nome**?

Noh-meh

Last name	Cognome
My **last name** is Russo.	Il mio **cognome** è Russo.

Coh-nyoh-meh

Profession	Professione
What is your **profession**?	Qual è la sua **professione**?

Proh-feh-seeoh-neh

Credentials	Referenze
Here are my **credentials**.	Ecco le mie **referenze**.

Reh-feh-rehn-tzeh

Skills	Competenze
These are my main **skills.**	Queste sono le mie **competenze** principali.

Kohm-peh-tehn-tzeh

As we know, the job market is nowadays different from how it was years ago. For many companies around the world, degrees and qualifications are not as important as they used to be. Therefore, a complete list of your knowledge and skills is very important.

Job title	Qualifica professionale
My **job title** is Manager.	La mia **qualifica professionale** è manager.

Kwah-lee-fee-kah proh-feh-seeoh-nah-leh

Job description	Descrizione del ruolo
That is not under my **job description.**	Questo non fa parte della **descrizione del ruolo.**

Dehs-kree-tzeeoh-neh dehl roo-oh-loh

Your job description needs to be clear. While your job title might be more generic, your job description should provide you a better idea of what is expected from you.

Milestone	Traguardo
What is your favorite **milestone?**	Qual è il tuo **traguardo** preferito?

Trah-gwahr-doh

As we have already said, where you worked in the past and for how long it doesn't matter anymore. What truly matters is what you have accomplished in the past. Choose wisely your greatest "traguardo" to prove your skills.

Manager	Manager
Congratulations! You are the new **manager.**	Congratulazioni! Sei il nuovo **manager.**

Mah-nah-gehr

This word is now used everywhere, so it is the same as in English: manager.

Congratulations! I am so happy for you!

You have been promoted pretty quickly, huh?

You know my motto: practice makes perfect! Let's look at our next conversation.

Manager:	*Hello! What can I do for you?*
	Salve! Cosa posso fare per lei?
Owen:	*Hello! I am looking for employment.*
	Salve! Sto cercando lavoro.
Manager	What is your name?
	Qual è il suo nome?
Owen:	*Owen Miller.*
	Owen Miller.
Manager	*Very well. What type of work are you looking for?*
	Molto bene. Che genere di lavoro sta cercando?
Owen:	*I would like anything. Even a temporary job.*
	Mi va bene qualsiasi cosa. Anche un lavoro temporaneo.

Manager	*Right. Did you bring your CV?*
	Va bene. Ha portato il suo CV?
Owen:	*Yes. Here it is.*
	Si. Eccolo qui.
Manager	*Very good. What are your major skills?*
	Molto bene. Quali sono le sue competenze principali?
Owen:	*I am good at logo design.*
	Sono bravo a disegnare loghi.
Manager	*What are your most relevant milestones from the past year?*
	Quali sono i traguardi più importanti che ha raggiunto nell'ultimo anno?
Owen:	*I won campaigns for logo refreshments in 5 major companies.*
	Ho vinto campagne per ricreare il logo in 5 grandi aziende.

Manager	*All right. We will call you for another interview.*
	Molto bene. La chiameremo per un'altro colloquio.
Owen:	*Do you have any vacancies?*
	Avete qualche posizione di lavoro?
Manager	*We have a job for a designer. It could turn into a permanent position.*
	Abbiamo una posizione per un designer. Potrebbe trasformarsi in un posto fisso.
Owen:	*That is great.*
	Sarebbe perfetto.
Manager	*Yes, it is. You would get an entry salary plus bonuses.*
	Si, lo è. Avrebbe uno stipendio iniziale più bonus.
Owen:	*Awesome. I will wait for your call.*
	Fantastico. Aspetterò la vostra chiamata.

We have already seen how an interview could start, but we are going to discuss that further in the next chapter. After all, you have to be ready for your next role.

www.LearnLikeNatives.com

Chapter 10 – Learn, Lead, Invest

As the title of this chapter suggests, now is the time to learn to lead. It's time to shine in your job interview. This is the moment to talk about your ambition, show how good you are at planning and projecting, and demonstrate why you will be a great fit. To do so, we will need to introduce a new tense: the future.

First verb: "to learn" – "imparare". As you will see, this verb is part of the first conjugation and its root is "impar-".

Eem-pah-rah-reh

Remember, you need to identify the root and then change the ending depending on the conjugation. For the verb "imparare", the root is "impar-".

To learn	Imparare	Root	Termination
I will learn	Io imparerò	Impar-	Are changes to "erò"
You will learn	Tu imparerai		Are changes to "erai"

He/She/It will learn	Lui/Lei/Egli imparerà		Are changes to "erá"
We will learn	Noi impareremo		Are changes to "eremo"
You will learn	Voi imparerete		Are changes to "erete"
They will learn	Loro impareranno		Are changes to "eranno"

Again, let's take a moment to repeat it all: Eem-pah-rah-reh

I will learn a lot in this company.	Io imparerò molto in questa azienda.
He will learn from this experience.	Lui imparerà da questa esperienza.
We will learn through hard work.	Noi impareremo attraverso il duro lavoro.
They will learn a lot.	Loro impareranno un sacco.

Now I think it's time to move to the second conjugation: verbs ending in "ere".

From a hiring perspective, "to lead" is a very important verb. Being able to lead is a well-appreciated skill for most recruiters, especially if you are applying for a managerial position.

The root for the verb "dirigere" is "dirig-".

To lead	Dirigere	Root	Termination
I will lead	Io dirigerò	Dirig-	Ere changes to "erò"
You will lead	Tu dirigerai		Ere changes to "erai"
He/She/It will lead	Lui/Lei/Egli dirigerà		Ere changes to "erá"
We will lead	Noi dirigeremo		Ere changes to "eremo"
You will lead	Voi dirigerete		Ere changes to "erete"
They will lead	Loro dirigeranno		Ere changes to "anno"

Dee-ree-jeh-reh

You will lead this project.	Tu dirigerai questo progetto.

She will lead this department.	Lei dirigerà questo dipartimento.
We will lead the first part of the conference.	Noi dirigeremo la prima parte del convegno.
They will lead us to success.	Loro ci dirigeranno al successo.

The best thing about a job interview is that you will be required to talk about yourself. Therefore, it is important to know all the different conjugations as you may want to talk about your plans for specific people or departments. Your main goal, however, should be learning to talk about yourself.

Now let's see a verb from the third conjugation: investire – to invest.

To invest	Investire	Root	Termination
I will invest	Io investirò	Port-	Ire changes to "irò"
You will invest	Tu investirai		Ire changes to "irai"
He/She/It will invest	Lui/Lei/Egli investirà		Ire changes to "irá"

We will invest	Noi investiremo		Ire changes to "iremo"
You will invest	Voi investirete		Are changes to "irete"
They will invest	Loro investiranno		Are changes to "iranno"

Io investirò – Ee-oh een-vehs-tee-roh

Now, let's see some examples.

I will invest in the company.	Io investirò nella compagnia.
He will invest many resources.	Lui investirà molte risorse.
We will invest in the personal training of our employees.	Noi investiremo nella formazione dei nostri dipendenti.
They will invest in technology.	Loro investiranno nella tecnologia.

The next verb we really need to look at is the verb "to be" - essere. Thanks to this verb, you can create the basic structure of most sentences. "Futuro semplice" is the most commonly used tense for the future. As usual, we will see a comparison between "essere" (to be) and "stare" (to stay)

To be	Essere	To stay	Stare
I will be	Io sarò	I will stay	Io starò
You will be	Tu sarai	You will stay	Tu starai
He/She/It will be	Lui/Lei/Egli sarà	He/She/It will stay	Lui/Lei/Egli starà
We will be	Noi saremo	We will stay	Noi staremo
You will be	Voi sarete	You will stay	Voi starete
They will be	Loro saranno	They will stay	Loro staranno

First, let's practice with the future tense of "essere".

I will be the leader of this project.	Io sarò il leader di questo progetto.
He will be a great asset to this team.	Lui sarà una risorsa fantastica per questa squadra.

This software will be great for us.	Questo software sarà perfetto per noi.
They will be ready for everything.	Loro saranno pronti per tutto.

Now, a few examples with the future tense of "stare".

I will be in a lead position this time.	Questa volta io starò in un ruolo dirigenziale
He will be waiting for your instructions.	Lui starà aspettando le tue istruzioni.
This job will be waiting for you.	Il lavoro starà aspettando te.
We will be in a meeting for the next hour.	Noi staremo in riunione per la prossima ora.

You can see that in Italian, the words "will be" are combined in a simple idea: "essere" or "stare". This is the Italian conjugation of the verb "to be", used to indicate things that will happen in the future.

Thanks to this verb, you can form a sentence and talk about your plans for the future.

"With these changes, we will be the first company in our field."

"Con questi cambiamenti, saremo l'azienda leader nel nostro settore."

Now, it is time to learn how to conjugate one more verb. Last but not least: "avere".

To have	Avere
I will have	Io avrò
You will have	Tu avrai
He/She/It will have	Lui/Lei/Egli avrà
We will have	Noi avremo
You will have	Voi avrete
They will have	Loro avranno

"To have" is a very useful verb as it is an auxiliary verb that helps us build new tenses and more complex sentences, as you have seen.

Yes, I understand how you feel. I can almost hear you moaning. No worries. We will see a few more practical applications in the next dialogue.

Mr. King (Sr. King):	*Hello. Are you Leo Mitchell?*
	Salve! È lei Leo Mitchell?
Leo:	*Good afternoon. Yes, I am.*
	Buon pomeriggio. Si, sono io.
Mr. King:	*Perfect. Please, come with me.*
	Perfetto. Per favore, mi segua.
Leo:	*Sure.*
	Certamente.
Mr. King (Sr. King):	*Tell me, Leo. If we hire you, what will you bring to the company?*
	Mi dica, Leo. Se la assumiamo, cosa potrà offrire all'azienda?
Leo:	*I will bring 10-years of experience in conflict and risk management.*
	Porterò i miei 10 anni di esperienza nella gestione dei conflitto e del rischio.

Mr. King (Sr. King):	*According to your knowledge, when will the updates be made?*
	In base alla sua conoscenza, quando crede saranno effettuati gli aggiornamenti?
Leo:	*I will have updates done within the first semester of 2020.*
	Completerò gli aggiornamenti entro il primo semester del 2020.
Mr. King (Sr. King):	*What will you need to achieve that?*
	Di cosa avrà bisogno per ottenere questo risultato?
Leo:	*I will need a team, including two technicians.*
	Avrò bisogno di una squadra, che include due tecnici.
Mr. King (Sr. King):	*Very well. When will you start?*
	Molto bene. Quando potrà iniziare?
Leo:	*Next week will be okay.*
	La prossima settimana andrà bene.

I hope you can now better understand how the future tense works. All languages are about structure and, even if some are more complex than others, it will become natural with time and practice. By the way, how is your new office?

Chapter 11 – New Job, New Life

I always feel a bit uncomfortable the first time I am in a new place, especially if it is going to be my new work environment! Of course, I also think is great to meet new people, build friendships, and more generally have the chance to network with other peers.

You won't have to worry as we are here to prepare you for what is coming. Do you want to join me?

Please, join me in your new office.

Office	Ufficio
This is your **office.**	Questo è il tuo **ufficio.**

Ooh-fee-choh

Computer	Computer
Your **computer** is ready to use.	Il tuo **computer** è pronto all'uso.

Kohm-pooh-terh

Database	Database
I granted you access to this **database.**	Ti ho concesso l'accesso a questo **database.**

Dah-tah Bah-zeh

Software	Software
We have the best **software** to manage our database.	Abbiamo il **software** migliore per gestire il nostro database.

Pro-gra-ma

Yes! You are right! All these words are the same in English and in Italian! What a piece of cake!

Keyboard	Tastiera
This is a nice **keyboard.**	Questa è una buona **tastiera.**

Tah-tztee-eh-rah

Monitor	Schermo
I need a larger **monitor.**	Ho bisogno di uno **schermo** più grande.

Skehr-moh

Alternatively, you can use the same word: "monitor".

Mouse	Mouse
My **mouse** is ergonomic.	Il mio **mouse** è ergonomico.

www.LearnLikeNatives.com

When talking about computer, most words remain the same.

Hard drive	Disco rigido
That is a 2-terabyte **hard drive.**	Quello è un **disco rigido** da 2 terabytes.

Dees-coh ree-gee-doh

File	File
You will find all that you need in the **file.**	Troverai tutto quello di cui hai bisogno in quel **file.**

This is the same as it is in English, same pronunciation "file".

Document	Documento
I already sent that **document.**	Ho già inviato quel **documento.**

Doh-coo-mehn-toh

Report	Relazione
I will send the **report** this afternoon.	Invierò la **relazione** questo pomeriggio.

Reh-lah-tzeeoh-neh

Coordinate	Coordinare

250

www.LearnLikeNatives.com

| We need to **coordinate** that meeting. | Dobbiamo **coordinare** quella riunione. |

Cohr-dee-nah-reh

| Desk | Scrivania |
| This is a nice **desk.** | Questa è una bella **scrivania.** |

Skree-vah-nee-ah

| Department | Dipartimento |
| I work for the Human Resources **department.** | Io lavoro nel **dipartimento** delle risorse umane. |

Dee-pahr-tee-mehn-toh

| Coworker | College di lavoro |
| I had lunch with a **coworker.** | Ho pranzato con un **collega di lavoro.** |

Coh-leh-gah dee lah-voh-roh

See how most of these words are either the same o very similar to the words in English?

Are you looking forward to putting what we have just learned into practice? That's fantastic! Let's do this!

Eli: *How do you like your new office?*

Cosa ne pensi del tuo nuovo ufficio?

Jace: *I like it a lot. I think I will need another monitor to split screens.*

Mi piace molto. Ma penso avrò bisogno di un altro monitor per dividere le schermate.

Eli: *Most coworkers do. We can coordinate that with the IT Department.*

Molti colleghi hanno fatto la stessa richiesta. Parleremo con il dipartimento IT per averne uno.

Jace: *Perfect. Thank you. I love my desk.*

Perfetto. Grazie. Adoro la mia scrivania.

Eli: *Yes. We invest in computers, software, and great equipment.*

Si. Investiamo in computer, software e attrezzatura all'avanguardia.

Jace: *When are you expecting to have the files you requested?*

Quando desideria avere i file che hai richiesto?

Eli: *Tomorrow is fine.*

Domani va bene.

Jace: *Good. I just have to add a few documents.*

Ok, ho solo bisogno di aggiungere qualche altro documento.

Eli: *Great, Jace! I think you will be a great addition to our team.*

Benissimo, Jace! Credo sarai una grande risorsa per la nostra squadra.

Jace: *Thank you for trusting in me. I will not let you down*

Grazie per avermi dato fiducia. Non vi deluderò.

How was your first day on the job? Are you already familiar with the coffee machine? You'd better work hard as you are going to be very busy soon.

www.LearnLikeNatives.com

A Quick Message

A quick message before we start the final chapter of this book.

"No one can whistle a symphony. It takes a whole orchestra to play it." –

H.E. Luccock

Do you want to be part of the orchestra of the Learning Italian community?

Here is how:

If you're enjoying this book, I would like to kindly ask you to leave a brief review on Amazon.

Reviews aren't easy to come by, but they have a profound impact in supporting my work. This way, I can keep creating new content to help the whole community at my very best.

I would be incredibly thankful if you could just take a minute to leave a quick review on Amazon, even if it's just a sentence or two!

www.LearnLikeNatives.com

It's that simple!

Thank you so much for taking the time to leave a short review on Amazon.

The community and I are very appreciative, as your review makes a difference.

Now, let's get back to learning Italian!

Chapter 12 – Bring Home the Bacon

You have been looking forward to this day for so long. You got yourself a new job, a new office and colleagues, and now it is time to start working for your future and make some money. As usual, let's start with the basics.

Meeting	Riunione
We have everything ready for the **meeting.**	Abbiamo tutto pronto per la **riunione.**

Ree-ooh-nee-oh-neh

Sell	Vendere
We plan to **sell** when it reaches $95.	Abbiamo intenzione di **vendere** quando raggiunge $95.

Vehn-deh-reh

Take your time to practice that "r" sound.

Capital	Capitale

We need to raise **capital.**	Dobbiamo incrementare il **capitale.**

Kah-pee-tah-leh

Market	Mercato
The **market** is shifting.	Il **mercato** sta cambiando.

Mehr-kah-toh

How are your open vowels looking? "Ah" is a good sound to practice.

Stock market	Mercato azionario
The **stock market** could crash.	Il **mercato azionario** potrebbe crollare.

Mehr-kah-toh ah-tzeeoh-nah-ree-oh

Project	Progetto
The new **project** is very complex.	Il nuovo **progetto** è piuttosto complesso.

Proh-jeh-toh

Budget	Budget

www.LearnLikeNatives.com

| The available **budget** is 750k. | Il **budget** disponibile è di 750k. |

Same as in English, that's great, right?

| Presentation | Presentazione |
| I'll have the **presentation** ready by 1 pm. | Finirò la **presentazione** prima di l'una. |

Preh-sehn-tah-tzeeoh-neh

| Supply | Offerta |
| The **supply** is decreasing for some commodities. | L'**offerta** di alcune materie prime sta diminuendo. |

Offer-ta

| Demand | Domanda |
| People **demand** new solutions. | La gente **domanda** nuove soluzioni. |

Doh-mahn-dah

| Experience | Esperienza |
| I have 7 years of professional **experience.** | Ho 7 anni di **esperienza** professionale. |

Ehs-peh-ree-ehn-tzah

Invoice	Fattura
I will send you my **invoice.**	Ti manderò la mia **fattura.**

Fah-too-rah

Credit	Credito
They have great **credit.**	Loro hanno un buon **credito.**

Creh-dee-toh

This is very similar to English, you just need to add a final "o".

Loan	Prestito
I will pay half of the **loan.**	Pagherò la metà del **prestito.**

Prehs-tee-toh

Taxes	Tasse
I have to calculate my **taxes.**	Devo calcolare le mie **tasse.**

Tah-seh

Investment	Investimento
It is a great **investment.**	È un buon **investimento.**

Een-vehs-tee-mehn-toh

Spend	Spendere
It is important to **spend** on quality.	È importante **spendere** in qualità.

Spehn-deh-reh

Save	Risparmiare
We can **save** up to 30%.	Possiamo **risparmiare** fino al 30%.

Rees-pahr-mee-ah-reh

Lose	Perdere
Sometimes you need to **lose.**	A volte bisogna **perdere.**

Pehr-deh-reh

Here we are. This is the last dialogue. In this session, we will practice what we have learned in the last three chapters. Are you ready? Don't be scared. I know you got this.

Mr. Reed (Sr. Reed):	*I am going to be clear: I want a company to protect my investment.*
	Sarò chiaro: voglio un'azienda che protegga i miei investimenti.
Mr. Evans:	*Perfect. I can offer you all my experience for that job.*
	Perfetto. Sono felice di offrirle tutta la mia esperienza.
Mr. Reed:	*What will be your strategy?*
	Quale sarà la tua startegia?
Mr. Evans:	*You have good credit. I plan to use a loan and increase the supply.*
	Lei ha un buon credito. Ho intenzione di usare un prestito per aumentare l'offerta.
Mr. Reed:	*How will I save capital that way?*
	Come risparmierò capitale in questo modo?
Mr. Evans:	*By covering for the demand, I expect a rise in the Stock Market.*

	Coprendo la domanda, prevedo un aumento del mercato azionario.
Mr. Reed:	*That will not do it alone.*
	Credo servirà più di questo.
Mr. Evans:	*I know. That is why we have a strategy to increase our market share by 3%.*
	Lo so. Per questo motive abbiamo una strategia per aumentare il valore dei nostri titoli di mercato del 3%.
Mr. Reed:	*Very well. I expect that you will have a great presentation for my board meeting.*
	Molto bene. Mi aspetto che lei abbia una buona presentazione per il mio consiglio di amministrazione.
Mr. Evans:	*You know I will. My budget projections do not lie.*
	Ne può stare certo. Le mie proiezioni di budget non mentono.
Mr. Reed:	*All right. I expect your invoice, then.*

                Molto bene. Attenderò la sua fattura, allora.

Mr. Evans: *I will be sending it tomorrow.*

                La manderò domani.

I would like to get your opinion. How was this chapter for you? And now ask yourself: how could you improve your knowledge? As I have been saying from the beginning, you will be able to learn the language by repeating all the lessons in this book. And practice is the only way to do it—repeat it all out will help a lot.

Conclusion

Congratulations on making it this far! We really are at the end of this book! You now have all the tools you need to speak Italian fluently.

There are no secrets or science but, of course, there is a method: practice, repeat, and repeat again! So, go for it. If you are still unsure about something, just go back to the relevant chapter and revise it. We are always here to help! Yet, I am sure you have already learned so much more than you realize!

Think about everything that we covered: we learned how to plan a trip, what to do if you or someone in your family get sick, how to move around the city, ask for directions, etc. We also introduced several verb tenses, to help you talk about the past and discuss the future.

We have also learned how to deal with business in Italian: we talked about how to present a CV and look for a new job. Moreover, we went through some commercial and business Italian in case you get a management position.

Do you realize how many new things you learned? You will now be able to communicate efficiently in different environments, from everyday life to business situations. I am so proud of you for coming so far!

You can find the rest of the books in the series, as well as a whole host of other resources, at LearnLikeNatives.com. Simply add the book to your library to take the next step in your language learning journey. If you are ever in need of new ideas or direction, refer to our 'Speak Like a Native' eBook, available to you for free at LearnLikeNatives.com, which clearly outlines practical steps you can take to continue learning any language you choose.

Nevertheless, it's not over yet!

Here is where the fun begins: try to watch your favorite movies or cartoons in Italian or maybe you could start with some famous TV series. Having Italian subtitles (yes with Italian subtitles, you can make it!) would definitely help. Movies and TV are extremely helpful to improve your Italian!

Once again, thank you so much for choosing this book. Hopefully, you will carry on your personal development using one of my other books in the near future!

Learn Like a Native is a revolutionary **language education brand** that is taking the linguistic world by storm. Forget boring grammar books that never get you anywhere, Learn Like a Native teaches you languages in a fast and fun way that actually works!

As an international, multichannel, language learning platform, we provide **books, audio guides and eBooks** so that you can acquire the knowledge you need, swiftly and easily.

Our **subject-based learning**, structured around real-world scenarios, builds your conversational muscle and ensures you learn the content most relevant to your requirements.
Discover our tools at *LearnLikeNatives.com*

When it comes to learning languages, we've got you covered!

www.ingramcontent.com/pod-product-compliance
Lightning Source LLC
Chambersburg PA
CBHW071727080526
44588CB00013B/1928